Cookie Craft

No-Bake Designs for
Edible Party Favors and Decorations

Cookie Craft
No-Bake Designs for
Edible Party Favors and Decorations

Barbara Williams
and Rosemary Williams

ILLUSTRATED WITH PHOTOGRAPHS BY
Barbara Williams

Holt, Rinehart and Winston / New York

Acknowledgment

The authors acknowledge with thanks the photographs
supplied by Safeway for the chocolate-covered
marshmallow cookie, the pastel-colored marshmallow
cookie, the fig bar, and the saltine, all from
their Busy Baker cookie line, and the pointed ice
cream cone from their Party Pride cookie line.

Library of Congress Cataloging in Publication Data

Williams, Barbara.
  Cookie craft.

  SUMMARY: Directions for creating forty-five party
favors and decorations from commercially prepared cookies.
1. Party decorations — Juvenile literature.
2. Holiday decorations — Juvenile literature.
3. Cookies — Juvenile literature.
[1. Party decorations.
2. Holiday decorations. 3. Cookies]
I. Williams, Rosemary, joint author.   II. Title.
TT900.P3W54   745.59'41
hc.   ISBN 0-03-020451-8
      77-3184   10 9 8 7 6 5 4 3 2

pbk.   ISBN 0-03-048971-7
      79-10356   10 9 8 7 6 5 4 3 2 1

To Joey, Tommy and Kim
who had a hand in this book

Contents

Introduction and General Suggestions

Recipes

Introduction and General Suggestions

Cookie Craft

Cookie craft is a new way to create party decorations that are both spectacular and delicious. Who would suspect that they're so easy? They are made from commercially-packaged cookies which are already baked. That's only the first reason you'll enjoy this new craft. As you follow the instructions in this book you'll also discover that cookie craft is fun and rewarding because

• there's no guesswork. Commercial cookies are more uniform in size and consistency than your own oven products.

• you can make your designs in advance. Commercial cookies don't get stale as fast as home-baked goods.

• materials are always handy—if not in your cupboard, as close as the nearest grocery store.

• completed craft items look more expensive than they really are. They'll cost less than comparable decorations and favors you can buy.

• your guests will exclaim over your originality and skill.

• they'll be surprised to see how much more can be done with a cookie or pretzel than with a cake.

• many items are as nutritious as they are attractive. Graham crackers and low-sugar wafers are the basic ingredients.

• decorative icing isn't absolutely necessary, as it is with cake decorating. You can eliminate most of it for weight-watchers and health-minded friends.

Cookie craft possibilities are endless. You'll find yourself looking at store displays with a new eye and creating exciting ideas of your own as you follow the instructions for the designs in this book.

The Cookies

Except for pretzels and animal crackers, which are not shown, these are the basic types of cookies called for in the recipes.

Double graham crackers
Single graham crackers
Vanilla wafers
Peanut creme cookies
Chocolate-covered marshmallow cookies
Pastel-colored marshmallow cookies
Scalloped buttercup cookies
Ice cream cones
Edible ice cream cups
Chocolate-covered fudge-filled cookies
Coconut bars
Fig bars
Saltine crackers
Sea toast crackers
Sugar wafers

Double graham cracker

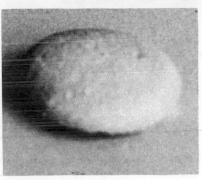

Single graham cracker

Vanilla wafer

Peanut creme cookie

Chocolate-covered
marshmallow cookie

Pastel-colored
marshmallow cookie

Scalloped buttercup cookie

Ice cream cone

Edible ice cream cups

Chocolate-covered
fudge-filled cookie

Coconut bar

Fig bar

Saltine cracker

Sea toast cracker

Sugar wafer

Cutting Cookies

Many of the designs in this book require that you cut commercially packaged cookies into smaller shapes. For best results choose cookies that are absolutely fresh. Set them flat-side down on a smooth cutting board (keep crumbs brushed carefully aside) and saw gently with a small serrated knife. Double-thickness cookies such as peanut cremes or graham crackers iced (glued) together, are less likely to crumble if you place a ruler on the cookie or cracker and, gently applying pressure, saw with a knife against the straight edge of the ruler.

Royal Icing— for Gluing and Decoration

The best icing both for gluing the cookies together and for decorating them with a tube is a simple, uncooked frosting made from egg whites and powdered sugar.

Ingredients
2 egg whites
1/2 teaspoon cream of tartar
3 cups powdered sugar
0-3 tablespoons water (as needed)
food coloring (optional)

Method
Place the egg whites and cream of tartar in a glass or metal (not plastic) bowl and beat at high speed with hand or

electric mixer for 1 minute. Gradually add sugar ¼ cup at a time and continue beating until frosting stands in fluffy peaks. The amount of water will depend upon the sizes of the eggs, the humidity, and purpose for which you need the icing. Use a thin, glossy frosting (2-3 tablespoons water) for covering a large surface and a thick, opaque frosting (0-1 tablespoon water) for pressing designs from a decorating tube.

Tinting icing

If you tint Royal Icing to match the color of the cookies you are working with, the seams won't show. They will look nicer and you won't have to cover them later with decorative icing.

To make brown icing, add equal amounts of red and green food coloring, using a drop at a time and stirring completely until you have the right color. If the brown seems too drab, add a drop or two of yellow coloring to brighten it.

Choose your own colors for decorative icing. Always add the coloring a drop at a time to be sure not to get it too dark.

Quantities needed

The above recipe will provide enough Royal Icing to cover the base of the train track and to glue six cars together. A double recipe will cover a larger structure such as the castle or haunted house. To make a few small items, such as trucks or wagons, cut the recipe in half (quantities smaller than half the recipe are impractical to prepare) and store leftover icing as described below.

Protecting and storing

Royal Icing works exceptionally well as a bond for cookies because it hardens rapidly when exposed to air. This means that you must also take precautions to keep it from hardening prematurely. Protect the icing in your bowl as you work by covering it lightly with a damp towel. Store any unused icing in your refrigerator in a plastic container with a tight-fitting lid.

Re-softening hard icing
If you neglect the precautions listed above and your Royal Icing begins to harden, you can beat it a second time with a hand or electric mixer, adding a few drops of water at a time until you regain the proper consistency. Restored icing works better for gluing than for decorating.

Graham Crackers

Besides being nutritious, inexpensive, and readily avail-able, graham crackers are the most versatile of all possible ingredients for cookie craft. You can cut them up and glue them back together in an endless variety of shapes—from the tiny cabin of a miniature tugboat to a multiple-story haunted house.

Purchasing hints
Many of the graham crackers you buy in any given package will be chipped or broken, and you will splinter still more as you work, so purchase twice as many as you will actually need for your craft project. (You can save the broken pieces for nibbling.) Select a brand which packages the cookies in double lengths (2 7/16'' x 4 7/8'') and scores them in the middle both lengthwise and crosswise for ease in cutting. Avoid stale crackers, which may be too warped or too dry to cut without breaking.

Effects of humidity

Excessive humidity or sudden changes in humidity (such as those caused by turning an air conditioner on and off) will cause graham crackers and cookies to sag. The results are not serious for small items such as the train cars, wagons, and flower carts, but the construction of large items such as the circus tent or castle is impractical and should not be attempted under humid conditions.

Large Graham Cracker Cube

A hollow, five-sided graham cracker cube measuring approximately 5″ in diameter provides the framework for the castle, cookie house, and haunted house designs in this book. After you have made one or two of these patterns you may want to create innovations of your own such as a school, church, gas station, courthouse, etc.

Materials needed for 1 large cube:
20 double graham crackers
Royal Icing (see page 15); one recipe will make several large
    cubes.
dull knife (for spreading icing)
serrated knife (for cutting crackers)
cutting board
ruler

To make sides
1. Spread 1 double graham cracker with Royal Icing and set it on a work table (see Figure 1).

Figure 1   Figure 2

2. Spread another double graham cracker with Royal Icing and set it next to the first cracker, sides touching (see Figure 2).
3. Lay 2 more double graham crackers on top of the first 2 in the opposite direction (sides touching) so that you have 1 large cracker measuring approximately 5″ x 5″ (see Figure 3).

Figure 3

4. Repeat steps 1, 2, and 3 to make 4 more large crackers (5 in all) for sides of the cube. Let dry at least 1 hour before proceeding.

To assemble

The instructions result in a cookie structure which is slightly oblong. If you desire a more perfect cube, disregard the suggestions which follow and use instead the ones for assembling the small cube by means of interlocking sides, on page 24.

1. Take each large cracker in turn and trim all 4 sides so that the 2 layers match evenly around the edges. Do not cut away any more of the crackers than necessary to make them even (see Figure 4).

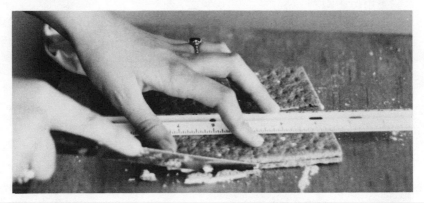

Figure 4

2. Lay 1 graham cracker on the cutting board. This is the base for the cube, around which you will glue the other sides (not ON it).

3. Gently remove a strip ½″ wide all along 1 end of the cracker by applying pressure against the cracker with a ruler and using its straight edge to guide your knife. This 4-sided base now has 2 sides which are wider than the other 2.

Figure 5   Figure 6

4. Take another cracker and spread a line of Royal Icing ¼''
   wide all along 1 edge (see Figure 5).
5. Glue the cracker at right angles to the base and outside it
   by setting its tip firmly on the cutting board (see Figure
   6).
6. Repeat steps 4 and 5 to glue another cracker to the other
   wide edge of the base.
7. Take another cracker and spread a line of Royal Icing ¼''
   wide along 3 edges in a U shape (see Figure 7).

Figure 7

8. Glue the cracker to the narrow edge of the base and against the 2 upright crackers, forming the third upright wall.
9. Repeat steps 7 and 8 to form the fourth upright wall of the cube.

Small Graham Cracker Cube

Unlike large cubes, which must be made in double thickness, small graham cracker cubes can be made either in single or double thickness. Double thickness cubes are recommended for the haunted house tower, where strength is more important than uniformity. However, single thickness cubes are recommended for the baby blocks on p. 103, since this design calls for daintiness in construction.

Materials needed for 1 double-thickness small cube:
10 single graham crackers
Royal Icing (p. 15); ½ recipe will make several small cubes.
dull knife (for spreading icing)
serrated knife (for cutting crackers)
cutting board
ruler

To make sides
1. Glue the 10 graham crackers together in pairs, making 5 double-thickness crackers measuring approximately 2 ½'' x 2 ½''. Let dry at least 1 hour before proceeding.

To assemble
1. Take each double-thickness cracker in turn and trim all 4 sides so that the two layers match evenly around the edges. Do not cut away any more of the crackers than necessary to make them even.
2. Lay 1 graham cracker on the cutting board. This is the base for the cube, around which you will glue the other sides (not ON it).
3. Gently remove a strip ¼'' wide all along the length and width of the base so that you end up with a cracker that is approximately square but ¼'' shorter and narrower than the side pieces (see Figure 1).

Figure 1

Figure 2   Figure 3

4. Take another cracker and spread a line of Royal Icing ¼''
    wide along the bottom and the right side.
5. Glue the second cracker outside the base and at right
    angles to it in an upright position by setting its tip firmly
    on the cutting board. Line up the left edges of the 2
    crackers so that the right edge of the upright wall on
    which you have placed Royal Icing extends beyond the
    edge of the base (see Figure 2).
6. Take another cracker and spread a line of Royal Icing ¼''
    wide along the bottom and the right side.
7. Glue the cracker outside the base and at right angles to it
    in an upright position by setting its tip firmly on the
    cutting board. The left tip of the cracker should attach
    firmly to the right edge of the previous cookie which has
    been spread with Royal Icing (see Figure 3).
8. Repeat steps 6 and 7 to glue 2 more upright sides to the
    base.
    To make a single thickness cube, omit the instructions for

Figure 4

gluing crackers together but follow the other steps listed above. You will need only 5 single crackers unless you want to fill in the empty sixth side of the cube (see Figure 4).

Graham Crackers as Boxes
and Other Shapes

Many of the designs in this book rely upon the technique of gluing graham cracker pieces together at right angles to form boxes of various sizes. The truck, wagon, flower cart, wheelbarrow, and luggage rack demonstrate the versatility of graham cracker construction, but even more patterns in this book can be adapted to graham crackers if you wish. The trains, the treasure chest, and Humpty Dumpty's wall can be made from graham crackers simply by cutting them to the dimensions of coconut bars, approximately $1\,5/8''$ x $2\,3/8''$.

Wheels

Scalloped buttercup cookies are the perfect size (2'' diameter) and shape (hole in middle) for wheels on graham cracker wagons, carts, and trucks. However they are not strong enough to support the vehicles, much less a load of candy or fruit, unless properly reinforced. Wherever buttercup wheels are called for in this book, reinforce and attach them as described below.

Materials needed for 4 reinforced wheels:
6 buttercup cookies (2'' diameter)
Royal Icing (p. 15); ½ recipe will make numerous wheels.
dull knife (for spreading icing)
serrated knife (for cutting cookies)
cutting board

Reinforcing wheels
1. Notice that each cookie has 8 scallops. Cut 1 cookie in half by dividing it between scallops—4 on each side. Hold the cookie in your left hand (if you are right-handed) and squeeze it gently from the edges toward the middle as you saw it gently with the knife held in your right hand.
2. Repeat step 1 to divide another cookie in half. You now have 4 whole cookies and 4 half cookies.
3. Take 1 half-cookie and spread it with Royal Icing. Glue it to a whole cookie, flat sides together, lining up the outside edges as smoothly as possible.
4. Repeat step 3 to make 3 more reinforced cookies.

Attaching Wheels

1. Turn a graham cracker wagon (or whatever vehicle you are making) upside down on a work table.
2. Spread the flat surface of the buttercup cookie with Royal Icing. (This is the top part of the wheel, the part not reinforced.) Also spread Royal Icing on the top ledge of the half cookie which provides the reinforcement.
3. Now turn the cookie upside down (as is the wagon) and glue it in place with the help of gravity. The ledge of the reinforcement will rest on the base of the wagon. Press the inside of the wheel which has been spread with icing firmly against the outside of the wagon and hold in place for a few seconds.
4. Repeat step 3 to attach 3 other wheels. Leave wagon and wheels upside down until thoroughly dry, at least 1 hour.

Recipes

Cookie Flowers

Even when it's snowing outside, you can sprout a bouquet of cookie flowers indoors in just a few minutes.

Materials needed for each flower:
1 scalloped buttercup cookie 2″ in diameter
1 large gumdrop measuring at least ¾″ at the base and
    preferably with a pointed top
Royal Icing (p. 15) Tint as desired.
decorator's tube
dull knife (for spreading icing)
sturdy green florist's wire approximately 9″ long
wire clippers, as needed
scissors, as needed
empty soda-pop bottle

Petals
Outline the scallops of the cookie as desired with icing from a decorator's tube. Let dry.

Center
1. A pointed gumdrop measuring ¾″ at the base will fit without adjusting the shape. A rounded gumdrop must be cut with scissors so most (but not all) of it will fit easily through the hole of the buttercup cookie.
2. Insert the gumdrop through the hole of the cookie from underneath. Spread a thick layer of Royal Icing on the wrong side of the cookie to hold the gumdrop in place. Proceed immediately to next step.

Stem

1. Insert 1 end of the wire through the moist icing into the gumdrop.
2. Set the flower upright in an empty soda-pop bottle to dry.

Arrangement

Arrange flowers as desired in an opaque container such as a teapot.

Caution: The gumdrop may contain dye from the florist's wire and should be removed if cookie flower is to be eaten.

Gumdrop Garden

A garden of colorful gumdrops will perk up each place setting at a party table on a drab day.

Materials needed for each garden:
1 round cookie 2 1/4'' in diameter
1 chocolate-covered fudge-filled cookie 1 3/4'' in diameter
5 straight pretzels approximately 2 1/4'' long
5 small gumdrops
Royal Icing (p. 15) Tint green.
dull knife (for spreading icing)
serrated knife (for cutting pretzels)
cutting board
decorator's tube
scissors
ice pick or metal skewer

Blossoms
Make a rosette from each gumdrop with clean scissors the way you would from a radish with a knife: Cut 5 slits low and around the outside of the gumdrop for the outside row of petals. Then cut 3 more slits slightly higher and toward the middle. Finally cut 1 slit at the top. Gently pull the petals out after you finish.

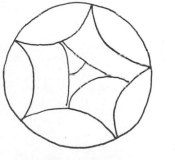

TOP VIEW

SIDE VIEW

33

Stems
1. Trim pretzels as needed so one is 2 1/4" and the rest are 2". The long pretzel is the stem for the flower in the middle.
2. Insert each pretzel in the base of a gumdrop rosette.

Base
1. With Royal Icing attach the chocolate-covered cookie to the center of the top of the larger round cookie. Let dry.
2. Using a sharp instrument like an ice pick or metal skewer, drill 5 holes in the chocolate cookie large enough to accommodate the pretzel stems. One hole in the center should go straight up. Four holes around the sides should slant outward.

Assembly
Insert the pretzel stems in the cookie base, using icing to hold them in place if necessary.

Decoration and Leaves
1. Add leaves on the stem of each rosette around the base of the flower with green icing and a decorator's tube.
2. Put a dot of green in the center of each flower with icing.
3. Trim the seam joining the two cookies on the base with green icing and a decorator's tube.

Humpty Dumpty

All the king's horses and all the king's men won't find a more delicious-looking Humpty Dumpty than this one made of marshmallow eclair cookies perched on a cocoanut bar wall.

Materials needed for 1 Humpty Dumpty and Wall:

1 small pastel-colored marshmallow cookie measuring 1 ¾'' in diameter

1 small chocolate-covered marshmallow cookie measuring 1 ¾'' in diameter

4 coconut bars

Royal Icing (p. 15) Tint some to match the coconut bars and the rest in a variety of shades for decoration.

decorator's tube

dull knife (for spreading icing)

serrated knife (for cutting cookies)

cutting board

4 regular 6'' pipe cleaners

Wall

1. Set 1 coconut bar on a working table with the flat side up.
2. Take 2 more coconut bars and trim one rounded edge from each along the length. Trim away only enough to give you a flat edge for gluing (see Figure 1).
3. Spread Royal Icing along the raw edges of the cookies you have just cut and glue them upright along the long

Figure 1   Figure 2   Figure 3

edges of the cookie on the working table. The furrowed sides of the upright cookies should face outward (see Figure 2).

4. Cut another coconut bar in half across the width.
5. Trim the remaining round side and the round bottom off each half cookie. You should now have 2 cookie pieces with raw, flat edges on the bottom and 2 sides but a round edge at the top.
6. Test each of the 2 half-cookie pieces for size by fitting them upright at the ends. If they don't fit smoothly between the 2 upright cookies already in position, trim them again with your knife.

Figure 4

7. Spread Royal Icing on the 3 raw edges of each cookie-half and glue them in place at the ends (see Figure 3). Let dry with open end on the table (see Figure 4).

Head and body
Using Royal Icing, glue the 2 marshmallow cookies together on their flat surfaces. Let dry.

Decoration
1. Using Royal Icing and a decorator's tube, make a wide frosting belt around Humpty's middle, covering the line

where the 2 cookies join. The chocolate cookie should be on the bottom to represent trousers.
2. Make a belt buckle for Humpty with icing in a contrasting color.
3. Make facial features for Humpty with icing and a decorator's tube.

Arms and legs
1. Bend each of the 4 pipe cleaners to represent an arm with a hand at the end or a leg with a foot at the end.
2. Insert the tips of the pipe cleaners in Humpty's body at the shoulder and hip joints.
3. Squeeze a small dab of frosting from the decorator's tube to cover the connections at shoulders and hips.

Assembly
Set the wall upright and place a small dab of icing on top to secure Humpty Dumpty in place. (Optional Wall Decoration: Trim the seams on Humpty's wall with decorative icing.)

Graham Cracker Wagon

A piece of colored paper converts a versatile graham cracker structure from a child's wagon to an old-fashioned covered wagon.

Materials needed for each wagon:
4 double graham crackers (For ease in measuring and cutting, purchase a brand which is scored both lengthwise and crosswise.)
4 reinforced buttercup wheels (p. 26)
4 Life Savers (optional)
Royal Icing (p. 15) Tint to match graham crackers.
Optional: ruler, colored paper, and scissors (for converting Child's Wagon to Covered Wagon).
dull knife (for spreading icing)
serrated knife (for cutting crackers)
cutting board
ruler

Bottom
1. With Royal Icing glue 2 double graham crackers together, one on top of another, and let dry.
2. With a gentle sawing motion and using the straight edge of the ruler to guide your knife, cut the double-thickness graham cracker into a 3 1/4" length. This is the bottom of the wagon.

Ends
1. Follow the scoring on a graham cracker to cut 2 pieces that should measure 1 1/4" x 2 3/8".

2. Set the bottom for the wagon on a working table and glue the end pieces against it (not ON it) by placing them upright from the work table.

Sides

1. Cut 1 double graham cracker along the scoring lengthwise.
2. Cut each of the 2 long graham cracker halves into 3 5/8'' lengths. These are the sides of the wagon.
3. Glue the side pieces against the bottom of the wagon (not ON it) and at right angles to the ends by setting them upright from the work table. Let wagon dry completely before proceeding.

Decoration (optional)

Using Royal Icing, glue a Life Saver over the hole of each reinforced buttercup wheel on the right side (the side opposite the reinforcement).

Handle

1. Insert the tip of a 6'' pipe cleaner in the center of one end of the wagon.

2. Bend the inserted tip ¼'' so it won't come out again.
3. Bend the opposite end of the pipe cleaner to resemble the handle of a child's wagon.

Attaching wheels to wagon
See p. 26 for reinforcing and attaching wheels.

Converting child's wagon to covered wagon
1. Measure and cut a rectangle of colored paper approximately 3 ¼'' x 7''.

2. Set the two ends of the paper inside the wagon, resting them on the bottom of the wagon at the far sides.

Graham Cracker Truck

Filled with dried apricots or apples, a graham cracker truck makes an unusual party favor which will delight both children and nutrition-minded parents.

Materials needed for each truck:

6 double graham crackers (For ease in measuring and cutting, purchase a brand which is scored both lengthwise and crosswise.)
4 reinforced buttercup wheels (p. 26)
2 Life Savers or other round candies for headlights
Royal Icing (p. 15)
dull knife (for spreading icing)
serrated knife (for cutting crackers)
cutting board
ruler
decorator's tube (optional)

Chassis

With Royal Icing glue 2 double graham crackers together, one on top of another, for a chassis which is long enough and strong enough to support the rest of the truck. Let dry completely before proceeding.

Back

1. Carefully cut 1 double graham cracker along the scoring, both lengthwise and crosswise, to make 4 cracker pieces measuring approximately 1 1/4" x 2 3/8".
2. Trim 2 of the 4 pieces so they are 1/4" shorter.

3. Using Royal Icing, glue the 4 cookie pieces upright on the chassis to make a box that covers half of the chassis. The longer pieces should go along the scoring in the middle (crosswise) and along the far edge. The shorter pieces should go on the edges between them.

Cab

REAR

1. Cut a small piece from a single graham cracker so it measures 2″ x 2 ³⁄₈″.
2. Using 2″ as the upright measurement of the rear of the cab, glue the cracker piece with Royal Icing on the chassis and flush against the back of the truck.

SIDES

1. From another cracker cut 2 pieces measuring 1″ x 2″.
2. Using 2″ as the upright measurement of the sides of the cab, glue the cracker pieces with Royal Icing on the side edges of the chassis and at right angles to the rear of the cab.

1. Cut a small piece from a single graham cracker so it measures 2'' x 2 3/8''.
2. Using 2'' as the upright measurement of the front of the cab, glue the cracker piece with Royal Icing on the chassis and at right angles to the side pieces, forming a second box on the chassis surface.

TOP

Cut a cracker along the lengthwise and crosswise scoring to get a piece measuring 1 1/4'' x 2 3/8''. With Royal Icing glue this in place as the top of the cab.

Engine

FRONT

1. Cut another cracker along the lengthwise and crosswise scoring to get a piece measuring 1 1/4'' x 2 3/8''.
2. Set the chassis on a working table and glue the front of the engine upright against it (not ON it) by setting the front piece upright from the work table.

TOP

1. Cut a cracker piece approximately 1 1/8'' x 2 3/8''.
2. Glue the cracker for the engine top in place by setting it on the front piece so it extends all the way to the front of the cab.

SIDES

1. Cut 2 cracker pieces approximately 3/4'' x 1''.
2. Glue them in the 2 holes at the sides of the engine.

Decoration

1. Glue 2 round candies on the front of the engine for headlights. Let truck dry completely.

45

2. Add icing trim along seams of truck with a decorator's tube, if desired. Avoid placing any trim under the places where you will install wheels, or they will not fit properly. Hold the wheels at the sides of the truck to get an approximate idea of those places you must avoid.
3. Apply decorative trim to reinforced buttercup wheels, if desired. Let decoration on truck and wheels dry completely before proceeding.

Attaching wheels to truck
See p. 26 for reinforcing and attaching wheels.

Wheelbarrow

Two sticks of candy and a chocolate-covered cookie perform magic on a simple graham cracker box.

Materials needed for each wheelbarrow:

3 double graham crackers (For ease in measuring and cutting, purchase a brand which is scored both lengthwise and crosswise.)
2 candy sticks approximately 4″ long
1 chocolate-covered, fudge-filled cookie approximately 1 3/4″ in diameter
Royal Icing (p. 15) Tint to match graham crackers.
dull knife (for spreading icing)
serrated knife (for cutting crackers and cookie)
cutting board
ruler

Bottom

1. Cut double graham cracker along crosswise scoring to make 2 single graham crackers.
2. Using Royal Icing, glue the single graham crackers together, one on top of another, and let dry. This is the bottom of the wheelbarrow.

Ends

1. Cut 1 double graham cracker along crosswise scoring to make 2 single graham crackers.
2. Set 1 single graham cracker aside to make the support piece later. Cut the other single graham cracker along the lengthwise scoring to make 2 pieces measuring 1 1/4'' x 2 3/8''. These are the end pieces.
3. Set the bottom for the wheelbarrow on a work table and glue the end pieces against it (not ON it) by placing them upright from the work table.

Sides

1. Cut a double graham cracker in half through the lengthwise scoring so you have 2 long crackers measuring approximately 1 1/4'' x 4 3/4''.
2. Cut these long crackers down into shorter lengths, approximately 2 3/4''. These are the sides.
3. Glue the side pieces against the bottom of the wheelbarrow (not ON it) and at right angles to the ends by setting them upright from the work table. Let wheelbarrow dry.

Wheel

1. Set the chocolate-covered cookie on a cutting board. Place the fingertips of your left hand (if you are right-handed) around it and squeeze from the rim toward the center of the cookie as you gently cut it with your right

hand. Remove a pie-shaped wedge equal to one-fourth of the cookie.

2. The cookie may break while you are cutting it, but you can probably glue it back together with Royal Icing so the break won't show. Let it dry completely.

Support

Cut a single cracker along the scoring and glue the halves together one on top of another. When dry, cut the double-thickness cracker into a piece approximately 3/4'' x 1 1/4''. This is the support for the wheelbarrow.

Assembly

1. Turn the box for the wheelbarrow upside-down on a work table and spread the entire bottom surface with a thick coat of Royal Icing tinted to match the graham crackers.
2. Spread Royal Icing on the 2 straight edges of the wheel where you removed a pie-shaped wedge. Glue the wheel around the corner of the box in the middle of one end. Part of it will rest on the bottom and part on the end. Gravity will hold it in place until it is dry.
3. On the opposite end from the wheel and in the center edge, glue the support piece in an upright position.
4. Glue 1 candy stick in place as follows. Set one end

touching the center of the wheel and let the other end fan out past the support piece and over the edge of the wheelbarrow.

5. Glue the other candy stick in a mirror image on the opposite side. The result will look like a modified letter *A* with the support piece representing the crossbar of the letter. Leave the wheelbarrow upside down until completely dry.

Flower Cart

Ornamental icing and artificial flowers provide the color for this unique table decoration.

Materials needed for each flower cart:

4 double graham crackers (For ease in measuring and cutting, purchase a brand which is scored both lengthwise and crosswise.)

4 reinforced buttercup wheels (p. 26)

4 Life Savers (optional)

1 scalloped sugar ring cookie 3'' in diameter

1 vanilla wafer 1 ½'' in diameter

3 candy sticks approximately 4'' long

Royal Icing (p. 15) Tint some in bright colors. Tint some to match the color of the graham crackers.

1 large gumdrop

dull knife (for spreading icing)

serrated knife (for cutting crackers)

cutting board

ruler

decorator's tube

artificial flowers

Umbrella holder

1. Break about 1″ from the end of 1 candy stick for the umbrella holder. (The umbrella looks better if it is not elevated too high.)
2. Insert one end of the candy stick upright in a large gumdrop. You must do this first because the gumdrop may split after it stands for a while. If this happens, fill up the crack with Royal Icing and cover the entire gumdrop with icing.

Umbrella

Spread a vanilla wafer with Royal Icing and glue it on the center top of the sugar ring cookie. Let dry.

Wheels

Using Royal Icing, glue a Life Saver over the hole of each reinforced buttercup wheel on the right side (the side opposite the reinforcement).

Bottom

1. Glue 2 double graham crackers together, one on top of another, and let dry.
2. With a gentle sawing motion and using the straight edge of the ruler to guide your knife, cut the double-thickness graham cracker into a 3″ length. This is the bottom of the cart. Notice that the flower cart is slightly larger than the wheel barrow and slightly smaller than the wagon. The reason is that the umbrella will look out of proportion to the cart if you make it too big or too small.

Ends

1. Follow the scoring on a graham cracker to cut 2 pieces measuring approximately 1 1/4″ x 2 3/8″.
2. Set the bottom for the flower cart on a work table and

glue the end pieces against it (not ON it) by placing them upright from the work table.

Sides
1. Cut 1 double graham cracker down the middle lengthwise.
2. Cut each of the 2 long graham cracker halves into 3 ⅜" lengths. These are the sides of the cart.
3. Glue the side pieces against the bottom of the cart (not ON it) and at right angles to the ends by setting them upright from the work table. Let flower cart dry.

Decoration
Put colored Royal Icing in a decorator's tube and trim the umbrella and wheels as desired. Let dry.

Handles

1. Turn the cart upside down on a work table and spread the entire bottom surface with Royal Icing tinted to match the crackers.
2. Set the 2 remaining candy sticks in the moist icing as handles for the flower cart. They should be parallel to each other near the sides of the cart and extending beyond one end about 1 ½". Let dry.

Attaching wheels to cart
See p. 27.

Attaching umbrella to cart

1. Set the flower cart upright on its wheels. It must be completely dry.

2. Glue the bottom of the gumdrop to the center of the flower cart. Let dry.

3. Fill the hole on the wrong side of the umbrella (the hole of the sugar ring cookie) with Royal Icing and set the umbrella on the upright candy stick. Let dry completely.

Flowers

Set artificial flowers in the cart, holding them in position, if desired, with mounds of Royal Icing tinted to match the crackers.

Fire Engine

What could excite youngsters more than a bright red fire engine . . . unless it's a fire engine they can eat! This peanut creme fire truck is a very special party decoration which you may want to award as the main prize. Set it on a piece of heavy cardboard so you can lift it from the bottom and avoid the risk of losing a wheel or two.

Unfortunately, peanut creme cookies are highly suscept-ible to humidity, and this design is not recommended for humid climates. See *Effects of Humidity*, p. 18.

Materials needed for each fire truck:
1 package (3) peanut creme cookies (purchase extra ones in
    case the cookies in the package are warped or broken)
12 chocolate-covered fudge-filled cookies
6 white Life Savers
2 red Life Savers
thin rope licorice
1 flat-bottomed, edible ice cream cup
Royal Icing (p. 15) Tint bright red, tan, and brown.
1 regular pipe cleaner
ruler
dull knife (for spreading icing)
serrated knife (for cutting cookies)
cutting board
decorator's tube

General instructions
Note that each peanut creme cookie is a sandwich composed of 1 flat cookie, 1 bulky cookie, and a peanut butter filling.

To glue these cookies together smoothly, you must trim the bulky cookie and the peanut butter filling away on many edges or entire surfaces.

Chassis
Set 1 whole peanut creme cookie flat side up on a work table.

Sides
1. Using a gentle sawing motion and the straight edge of the ruler to guide your knife, cut 1 peanut creme cookie in half lengthwise.
2. Spread tan Royal Icing along their cut edges and glue the two cookie halves upright on the outside edges of the chassis. Let dry.

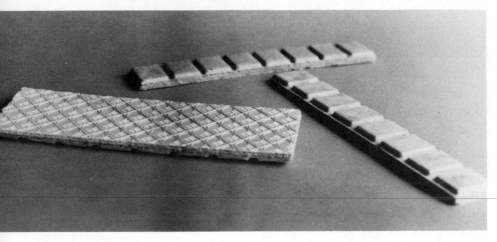

Engine

FRONT
Cut 1 cookie piece measuring approximately 1 ³/₄'' x 3 ¹/₄''. Trim the bulk from the edges as necessary and glue upright at one end of chassis.

Cut 1 cookie piece measuring 1 ¼″ x 3 ⅜″. Trim the bulk from the edges as necessary and glue at right angles to the engine front and resting on the sides.

Cab
Cut 5 cookie pieces for the cab, as shown in the diagram on the following page.

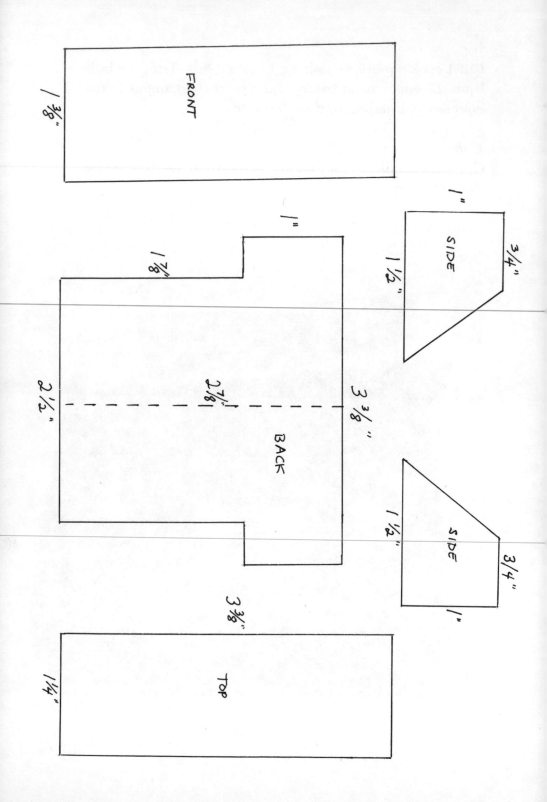

SIDES

Glue cab sides on the sides of the truck about ⅛ inch behind the engine top. Do not trim away bulk from cab sides.

BACK

Glue cab back upright behind cab sides. Do not trim away bulk from cab back.

FRONT

Trim away bulk from bottom and two sides of cab front and glue on the incline provided by cab sides.

Remove all of bulky layer from cab top and glue in position.

Wheels

1. Scrape chocolate from one flat side of each fudge-filled cookie to prepare for gluing. (Royal Icing does not adhere to chocolate.)
2. Glue the chocolate cookies together in pairs to make 6 wheels. The double-thickness is necessary to support the weight of the fire engine. Let dry.
3. Glue a white Life Saver on the top of each double cookie. Let dry.

Hose

1. Wind thin rope licorice into a circle about 2 ½'' in diameter to resemble a hose which has been rolled up.
2. Attach the licorice to a flat-bottomed ice cream cone with a small length of pipe cleaner bent into a U. Insert both ends of the U into the cone and twist from the inside. Trim pipe cleaner from the inside as necessary.
3. Spread Royal Icing around the rim of the cone and glue it upside down on the back of the truck.

Lights
Glue 2 red Life Savers to front of engine for lights.

Ladders
With brown icing and a decorator's tube, draw long ladders on each side of the fire engine.

Decoration
1. Draw windows on the cab with red icing and a decorator's tube.
2. Trim seams, as desired, with red icing and a decorator's tube.

Assembly
1. Trim one side of each wheel to provide a flat surface to support truck.
2. Trim the opposite side of each wheel to provide a flat surface for wheel to rest on.
3. Set wheels in position to support truck and put a dab of Royal Icing on the top of each.
4. Attach fire engine to wheels and let dry.

Treasure Chest

Guaranteed to delight young pirates (or just about anyone) is a cookie treasure chest filled with chocolate coins. Make it from coconut bars, as described here, or from graham crackers cut to approximately the same size (1 5/8'' x 2 3/8'').

Materials needed for each chest:
4 coconut bars
Royal Icing (p. 15) Tint to match coconut bars.
dull knife (for spreading icing)
serrated knife (for cutting cookies)
cutting board
wooden pencil or other small object

Bottom
Set 1 coconut bar on a work table with the flat side up. This is the bottom of the chest.

Sides
1. Set another coconut bar on a cutting board with the flat side down. Using a serrated knife and a gentle sawing motion, cut the cookie in half along its length. You now have two of the four sides you will need for the chest (see Figure 1).
2. Spread icing along the raw edges of the cookie halves

Figure 1

Figure 2

you have just cut and glue the two sides of the chest to the long edges of the bottom cookie (see Figure 2). The furrowed sides of the cookie halves should face outward.

3. Set another coconut bar on the cutting board with the flat side down, and cut it in half lengthwise, as before. You will need only 1 of these halves.

4. Take 1 half piece and cut it in half through the width to make 2 quarter pieces.

5. Trim the remaining round side (but not the top) off each quarter piece. You should now have 2 cookie pieces with raw, flat edges on the bottoms and sides but round edges on the tops.

6. Test both of the 2 cookie pieces for size by fitting them in place at the ends of the treasure chest. If they don't fit smoothly between the 2 sides already in place, trim them again with your knife.

7. Spread Royal Icing on the three raw edges of both small cookie pieces and glue them in position at the ends of the treasure chest.

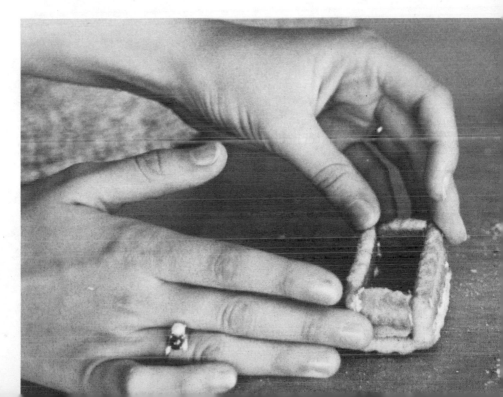

Lid

Take 1 whole coconut bar and spread it with Royal Icing on one long side. Glue it in place as the lid of the chest, propping it in an open position with a wooden pencil or other small object until the icing hardens.

Beach Hat

Less caloric than it looks, this charming beach hat is made from an ice cream cup set on a sugar-free cracker and adorned with icing from a decorator's tube.

Materials needed for each beach hat:
1 round sea toast cracker approximately 4 1/8″ in diameter
1 flat-bottomed edible ice cream cup 1 1/2″ at the base
Royal Icing in various shades (p. 15)
decorator's tube
dull knife (for spreading icing)

Crown
Take ice cream cup and break it piece-by-piece from the edge until it measures approximately 1 1/2″ high. This is the crown of the hat.

Brim

Set one 4 ⅛'' cracker on a working table. This is the brim of the hat.

Assembly

Spread Royal Icing on the broken edge of the ice cream cup and glue the cup upside down in the center of the cracker. Let dry.

Decoration

Trim the hat as desired with colored icing and a decorator's tube, making certain to cover the outside edge of the cracker.

Beach Goggles

All eyes at your party table will focus on zany beach goggles made from pipe cleaners and scalloped buttercup cookies.

Materials needed for each pair of goggles:
2 buttercup cookies
Royal Icing (p. 15)
3 standard pipe cleaners 6'' long or 1 long pipe cleaner at least 14'' (6'' pipe cleaners can be found in black or white in a tobacco store. 14'' pipe cleaners can be found in assorted colors in a craft-supply store.)
sturdy scissors (for cutting pipe cleaner)
ruler
decorator's tube (optional)

Frames
Set 2 buttercup cookies face down on a working table about ³/₈'' apart. These are the frames of the goggles.

Nose piece
1. Cut a 2'' length of pipe cleaner and bend it into a U. This is the nose piece for the goggles.
2. Using Royal Icing, attach the nose piece to each buttercup cookie so it connects them near the top, resembling the nose piece on a pair of glasses. Most of each side of the U should be attached to a cookie for maximum strength. Hold bonds in place until nearly dry.

Ear pieces
1. Cut 2 pieces of pipe cleaner 6'' long.
2. Using Royal Icing, glue about ¹/₂'' of the end of each pipe

cleaner to a cookie with the rest of the pipe cleaner extending straight out. These ear pieces should be attached near the tops of the cookies at the spots where ear pieces are attached to real glasses. Hold in place until dry.

Decoration
Turn goggles face up and outline cookies as desired with colored icing and a decorator's tube. Let dry.

Finishing goggles
Bend pipe cleaners to resemble the ear pieces on real glasses.

Bell

Suitable for a wedding party, a New Year's Eve party, or almost any happy event is a table arrangement of cookie bells. Extra bells lying on their sides at each place setting enhance the festive appearance of the table.

Materials needed for each bell:
1 small marshmallow cookie 1 3/4'' in diameter
1 flat, round cookie 2 3/8'' in diameter
1 small gumdrop
Royal Icing (p. 15)
decorator's tube (optional)
thin florist's (covered) wire (optional)
dull knife (for spreading icing)
scissors
3/8'' ribbon (optional)

Assembly
Using Royal Icing, attach the marshmallow cookie on the center top of the round cookie.

Hanger (optional)
1. Cut a length of thin florist's wire 3 1/4''.
2. Twist the two ends of the florist's wire around each other for a length of about 1''. This should leave a loop in the opposite end of the wire, as shown in the photograph.
3. Spread Royal Icing on the twisted portion of the wire and insert the wire into the marshmallow cookie from the top so only the loop remains exposed. Let dry.

Shaping the bell
Spread Royal Icing over the sides and top of the bell, letting it touch the wire for the hanger. This will give the cookies a bell shape and also help keep the hanger in place. Let dry.

Clapper
1. Tip the bell on its side and spread Royal Icing over the bottom.
2. Attach a small gumdrop on the bottom center of the bell to resemble a bell clapper. Let dry.

Decoration (optional)
With a decorator's tube make a border of icing around the bottom of the bell. Let dry.

Ribbon (optional)
Cut a 3/8'' ribbon approximately 15'' long and tie a bow at the base of the hanger.

Caution: The top part of the bell may contain some dye from the florist's wire. Remove the top of the marshmallow cookie if the bell is to be eaten.

Die

Guests will feel lucky with one or several cookie dice stacked in the middle of a party table.

Materials needed for 1 die:
graham cracker cube (p. 18)
Royal Icing (p. 15)
20 round candies, chocolate or licorice
dull knife (for spreading icing)

Assembly

1. Cover five sides of a graham cracker cube with white Royal Icing.
2. While icing is still moist, arrange candies on the cube to resemble numbers on a die.

Flying Saucer

Space-minded youngsters may go into orbit over these.

Materials needed for each flying saucer:
1 round sea toast cracker approximately 4 1/8'' in diameter
1 large marshmallow cookie measuring 2'' in diameter
6 small gumdrops
Royal Icing (p. 15)
1 regular 6'' pipe cleaner
scissors (for cutting pipe cleaner)
sharp knife (for cutting gumdrops)
decorator's tube
dull knife (for spreading icing)

Assembly
Spread Royal Icing on the bottom of the marshmallow cookie and glue it in the center top of the large cracker. This is the basic structure of the flying saucer.

Antennae
1. Cut the pipe cleaner in half to make 2 antennae.
2. Bend the pipe cleaners slightly and stick them into the top of the marshmallow cookie.

Decoration
1. Using a decorator's tube swirl icing around the base of the marshmallow cookie.
2. Make a small puff of icing with the decorator's tube on top of the cookie where the pipe cleaners have been inserted. This will not only provide a decoration on top but will help hold the antennae in place.

Lights
1. Shorten the height of each gumdrop by cutting it at the base.
2. Glue the 6 gumdrops around the rim of the cracker as 6 evenly-spaced lights.

Fig bars trimmed at their edges and re-glued in various ways provide the many shapes of suitcase favors for a bon voyage party.

Materials needed for 1 suitcase:
1-4 fig bars (Purchase bars which are not concave and will lie flat on a table. The number of bars for each suitcase depends upon the shape you want to make.)
thin rope licorice
Royal Icing (p. 15)
sharp knife (for cutting bars and licorice)
dull knife (for spreading icing)
cutting board
2 straight pins
decorator's tube (optional)

Shaping the suitcase
The rounded edges of a fig bar are perfect for the top of a suitcase. If you want to make 1 tiny suitcase, you can leave a single bar intact except for trimming the bottom edge slight-

ly so the bar will stand upright. If you want to make a larger suitcase, you must glue 2, 3, or 4 bars together. To do so trim any edges flat before gluing them next to the edges on other bars.

Covering the suitcase
Spread the entire surface of the suitcase with a thin, glossy mixture of Royal Icing, tinted in a shade suggestive of luggage.

Handle
1. Cut a piece of licorice approximately 1 ½'' long.
2. Stick a straight pin through each end of the licorice ¼'' from the tip. Stick the pins all the way through to their heads.
3. While icing on the suitcase is still moist, insert the pins into the top of the fig bar suitcase. Place the pins close enough together so a half circle of licorice sticks in the air like the handle on a suitcase. Let dry.

Monogram
Add guest's initials, if desired, with a decorator's tube and icing in a contrasting color.

Luggage centerpiece
To make a luggage centerpiece like the one in the photograph, set the finished suitcases on graham cracker boxes of different shapes and sizes. (See p. 25.) Spread the boxes with thin, glossy Royal Icing and place the suitcases on them while the frosting is still moist. Be certain that your centerpiece is as attractive from the back as from the front if it will be seen from all angles.

Caution: Remove straight pins if the luggage is to be eaten.

Irish Hat

A low-sugar novelty for calorie counters is an Irish hat made from a cracker and a flat-bottomed, edible ice cream cup.

Materials needed for each hat:
1 round sea toast cracker approximately 4 1/8'' in diameter
1 flat-bottomed, edible ice cream cup 1 1/8'' at the base
Royal Icing (p. 15)
green gumdrop (optional)
green ribbon 1/2'' wide
green paper
scissors
dull knife (for spreading icing)
straight pin

Assembly
1. Spread Royal Icing around the rim of the ice cream cup and glue it upside down on the center top of the cracker. Let dry.
2. Cut a piece of green ribbon 10 1/2'' long and wrap it around the base of crown.
3. Attach ribbon to hat with a straight pin.
4. Cover the head of the pin, if you wish, by cutting a piece of gumdrop with your scissors and gluing it to the ribbon with icing.
5. Cut shamrocks from green paper and glue them to the crown.

Caution: Remove straight pins if the hat is to be eaten.

Windmill

As easy as they are breezy, windmills made from flat-bottomed, edible ice cream cups bring a suggestion of Holland to a party table.

Materials needed for each windmill:
2 flat-bottomed, edible ice cream cups measuring
  1 ½'' in diameter at the base
2 single graham crackers
4 sugar wafers measuring approximately ⅞'' x 1 ⅞''
1 small gumdrop
Royal Icing (p. 15)
decorator's tube or small candies
12 straight pins
dull knife (for spreading icing)

Base
Using Royal Icing, glue 2 single graham crackers together, one on top of another, and let dry. This is the base on which you will set the windmill.

Main structure
1. Spread Royal Icing on the bottom of 1 ice cream cup and glue it to the center of the base.
2. Spread Royal Icing around the top edge of the second ice cream cup and set it upside down on the first cup. Let dry.

Coating the structure (optional)
Cover the base and main structure with Royal Icing, if desired.

Vanes

1. Use 4 sugar wafers as 4 vanes for the windmill. Attach them with Royal Icing to the front of the top half of the main structure in the form of an X. Leave a square space approximately ⁷⁄₈'' x ⁷⁄₈'' in the center of the X.
2. Stick 2 or 3 straight pins through the center tip of each sugar wafer to keep it in place until the frosting dries. Do not remove pins.

Decoration

1. Glue a small gumdrop in the square space between the vanes.

2. Cover the pins with colored icing from a decorator's tube or glue small candies in place to hide them.
3. Add other decorative icing as desired.

Caution: Remove straight pins if the windmill is to be eaten.

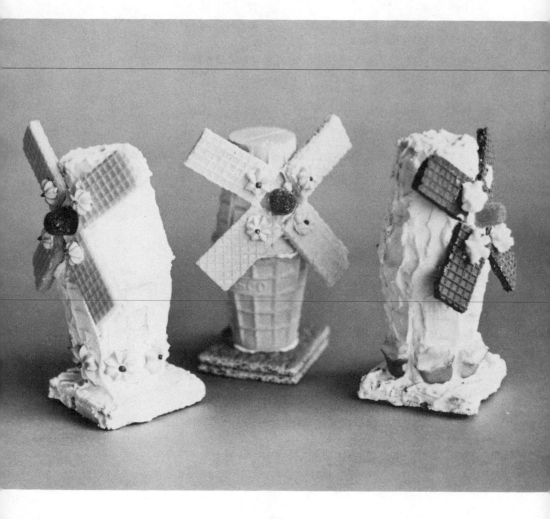

Lighthouse

To guide tugboats, sailboats, or other small craft to safety, make a lighthouse from 3 flat-bottomed ice cream cups.

Materials needed for each lighthouse:
2 single graham crackers
2 flat-bottomed, edible ice cream cups measuring 1 1/4'' in diameter at the base
1 flat-bottomed, edible ice cream cup measuring 1 1/2'' in diameter at the base
Royal Icing (p. 15)
dull knife (for spreading icing)

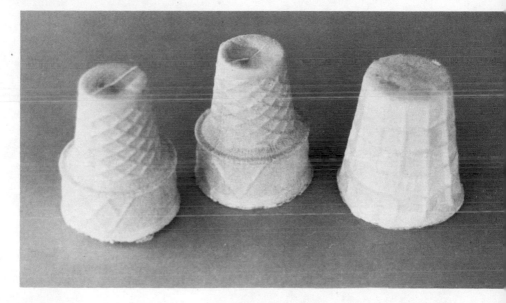

Base
Using Royal Icing, glue 2 single graham crackers together, one on top of another, and let dry. This is the base on which you will set the lighthouse.

Main structure

1. Take 1 of the 2 matching cups and spread Royal Icing around the top edge. Glue the cup upside-down on the graham cracker base.
2. Take the other matching cup and spread Royal Icing on the bottom. Glue it right-side-up on top of the first cone.

Light tower

1. Take the cup with the larger base and break it from the top, bit by bit until it stands approximately 1'' high.
2. Glue the cup you have just broken upside down inside the top cup of the main structure.

Tugboat

Sturdy tugboats made from coconut bars and graham crackers look ready for work or for eating.

Materials needed for each tugboat:
4 double graham crackers
5 coconut bars
4 Life Savers
Royal Icing (p. 15) Tint to match coconut bars.
sharp knife
dull knife (for spreading icing)
serrated knife (for cutting cookies)
ruler
decorator's tube (optional)
cutting board

Deck
1. Glue 2 double graham crackers together, one on top of another, with Royal Icing and let dry.
2. With the point of a sharp knife, mark the double cracker in preparation for cutting it in the shape illustrated in the diagram on the next page.

3. Set the double cracker on a cutting board and trim it to size as marked, sawing it gently back and forth and using the straight edge of the ruler to guide your knife.

Cabin

CENTER
1. Glue 2 single graham crackers together, one on top of another, and let dry.

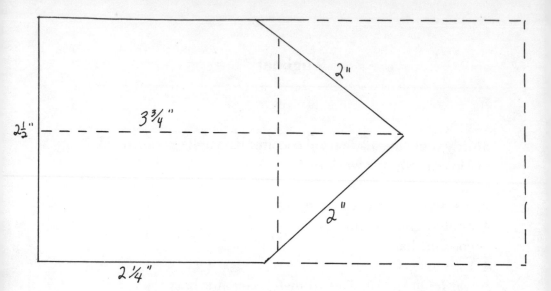

2. Set the double-thickness cracker on a cutting board and cut it to a square measuring 1 ¼'' x 1 ¼''.

ENDS

1. From a single-thickness graham cracker cut 2 pieces measuring 1 ¼'' x 1 ¼''.
2. Set the double-thickness square on a work table.
3. Using Royal Icing, glue the two ends against the double-thickness cracker (not ON it) by setting them upright from the working table.

SIDES

1. From a single-thickness graham cracker cut 2 pieces measuring 1 ¼'' x 1 ½''.
2. Using Royal Icing, glue the two sides against the double-thickness cracker (not ON it) and at right angles to the ends by setting them upright from the work table. Let cabin dry while you proceed.

Sides of tugboat

Make sides for the tugboat by gluing 5 coconut bars against the 5 sides of the deck (not ON it). In order for the cookies to fit together smoothly at each corner, the ends must be cut at about a 45° angle. This is particularly important for the 2 cookies at the front of the boat. Set each cookie in turn on the cutting board with the furrowed side down and cut its two ends with your knife slanting downward toward the outer edge of the cookie.

Decoration
Trim seams of cabin and tugboat, as desired, with Royal Icing and a decorator's tube.

Assembly
Spread icing around edges of cabin and glue upside down on deck of tugboat.

Smoke stack
Glue a stack of 4 Life Savers on the top of the cabin.

Sailboat

As appetizing as "the good ship lollipop," this graham cracker sailboat sports a peppermint-stick mast and crisp red trim.

Materials needed for each sailboat:
6 double graham crackers
1 single graham cracker
1 candy stick about 5'' tall and 1/2'' in diameter
1 mint or other soft candy 1'' in diameter
Royal Icing (p. 15) Tint some to match graham crackers, the
    rest bright red.
white construction paper
scissors
red magic marker
ruler
dull knife (for spreading icing)
serrated knife (for cutting crackers)
cutting board
decorator's tube
glue

Sides
1. Glue 2 double graham crackers together, one on top of another, with tan icing. Let dry.
2. Cut double-thickness cracker in half lengthwise to make the two sides of the boat.

End
1. Cut 1 single graham cracker in half along the scoring.

2. Glue the 2 halves together to make a double-thickness cracker for the end of the boat.

Bottom

1. Spread 1 double graham cracker with tan icing and set it on a work table.
2. Spread another graham cracker with icing and line it up evenly with the first, sides touching.
3. Lay 2 more double graham crackers on top of the first 2 in the opposite direction (sides touching) so that you have 1 large cracker measuring approximately 5'' x 5''. Let dry.

Assembly

1. Using Royal Icing glue the sides and end of the boat together in a triangle, beveling the corners as necessary so they will fit snugly.
2. Glue the triangle on top of the 5'' x 5'' cracker you have prepared for the bottom. (The edges of the bottom will extend beyond the triangle.) Let dry.
3. Trim the edges of the bottom to fit the shape of the boat.

Mast

1. With the point of a knife, make an indentation in the mint candy large enough to accommodate the candy stick.
2. Glue candy stick in mint with icing. Let dry.
3. Glue candy mint to bottom of boat with icing. Let dry.

Sail

1. From white construction paper cut a triangle with one perpendicular side measuring 5'', a horizontal bottom measuring 3 1/2'', and a connecting side between them.

2. Border the sail with red, using a ruler and magic marker.
3. With real glue attach the perpendicular side of the triangle sail to the candy stick mast.

Decoration

Decorate top edges of boat and all seams as desired with red Royal Icing and a decorator's tube.

Raft

Relax and enjoy a casual but unique party decoration—a raft made from giant pretzel sticks. A graham cracker shelter reinforces the construction of pretzel logs.

Materials needed for each raft:
9 pretzel sticks approximately ½'' in diameter and 7'' long
4 double graham crackers
1 saltine cracker
Royal Icing (p. 15) Tint to match pretzels.
dull knife (for spreading icing)
serrated knife (for cutting crackers)
cutting board
ruler

Raft
Using Royal Icing, glue 8 pretzels together side by side. Let dry.

Shelter

TOP
1. Glue 2 double graham crackers together one on top of another. Let dry.
2. Set the double-thickness cracker on a cutting board. With a gentle sawing motion and using the straight edge of a ruler to guide your knife, cut a rectangle measuring approximately 1 ¾'' x 3 ¼''. This is the top of the shelter, but for the time being, you will work with it on the bottom.

ENDS

1. Cut 2 graham cracker pieces measuring 1 ½'' x 1 ¾''. The shorter measurement will be the height of the shelter.
2. Set the top of the shelter on a working table. Spread Royal Icing along one long side of each cracker piece you have just cut and glue both of them in place as ends of the shelter by setting them upright against the top (not ON it).

SIDES

1. Cut 2 graham cracker pieces measuring 1 ½'' x 3 ½''. The shorter measurement is the height.
2. Spread Royal Icing along one long edge of each cracker piece and glue both of them in place as sides of the shelter by setting them upright against the top (not ON it). The shelter is now finished but upside-down. Leave it in this position until icing dries.

Assembly

Spread icing around the exposed edges of the upside-down shelter. Now turn it over and glue it in position about 1 ½'' from one end of the raft.

Mast

Take the remaining pretzel stick and spread Royal Icing on the bottom and up one side about 1 ½''. Glue it in place behind and against the shelter.

Sail

Glue a saltine cracker on the mast for a sail.

97

Parasol

Whenever showers come your way, you can brighten a party table with miniature parasols decorated with Royal Icing.

Materials needed for each parasol:
1 scalloped sugar ring cookie 3″ in diameter
1 vanilla wafer 1 ½″ in diameter
Royal Icing (p. 15) Tint in pastel shades.
1 sturdy pipe cleaner 6″ long
dull knife (for spreading icing)
decorator's tube

Assembly
1. Spread the bottom of a vanilla wafer with Royal Icing and glue it on the center top of the sugar ring cookie.
2. While icing is still slightly moist, insert one end of a pipe cleaner from the underneath side through the hole of the sugar ring and part way into the vanilla wafer.
3. Turn the parasol upside-down to dry (vanilla wafer on bottom, pipe cleaner upright in air).
4. When frosting is completely dry, bend pipe cleaner so that top of parasol lies flat enough for you to manipulate a decorator's tube with ease.
5. Trim parasol as desired with Royal Icing tinted in pastel shades. Let dry completely.
6. Bend pipe cleaner to resemble the handle on a parasol.

Cradle

As charming as they are easy to make, dainty cookie cradles will add to the joy of "infanticipating."

Materials needed for each cradle:
1 coconut bar
3 small pastel-colored marshmallow cookies measuring 1 ¾'' diameter. (Select a brand of cookie that is firm rather than soft, or allow cookies to get slightly stale.)
Royal Icing (p. 15) Tint in pastel shades.
dull knife (for spreading icing)
serrated knife (for cutting cookies)
cutting board
decorator's tube

Rockers
1. Cut 1 marshmallow cookie evenly through the center to make 2 halves.
2. Set a coconut bar on a work table, furrowed side up.
3. With cut ends down and flat sides facing each other, attach each half of the marshmallow cookie to either end of the coconut bar with Royal Icing.

4. When icing dries, turn coconut bar upright on its rockers and test it for stability. Trim the very tips of the rockers as necessary so the cradle rests flat on the table.

Hood
1. Set a marshmallow cookie flat side down on the cutting board.
2. Trim off a small piece of the cookie on one side so that it will rest flat when you turn it on its side.
3. Glue the cut edge of the marshmallow cookie to the far end of the coconut bar to make a cradle hood (see Figure 1).

Figure 1   Figure 2

Bed
1. Set the last marshmallow cookie flat side down on the cutting board.
2. Trim off a small piece of the cookie on one side (as before) so that it can rest flush against the hood of the cradle.
3. Trim off a small piece from the top of the rounded cookie so that it will lie flat when turned upside-down.
4. Now turn the cookie over with the original flat surface at the top. Glue this bed for the cradle on the coconut bar so that the cut side rests flush against the hood (see Figure 2).

Trimming

1. Spread the top of the bed and the inside of the hood with pastel icing.
2. Make a frosting ruffle around the hood with pastel icing from a decorator's tube.
3. Add flowers or ribbons as desired with icing and a decorator's tube.

Blocks

A stack of alphabet blocks makes an attractive centerpiece by itself or as a display rack for small cookie craft objects or toys. Cover it with white icing trimmed in pastels like the stack in the photograph for a baby shower or use darker icing for a child's birthday party.

The cardboard base which supports the blocks in the photograph is the kind which bakeries use under their cakes. If you cannot buy a similar round cardboard from a bakery, pizza house, or wholesale outlet, make your own from heavy white cardboard.

Materials needed for a stack of blocks:
6 small graham cracker cubes (p. 22)
Royal Icing (p. 15) Tint as desired.
sturdy round cardboard 12'' in diameter
dull knife (for spreading icing)
decorator's tube

Assembly
1. Cover 3 blocks with Royal Icing and set them on the cardboard base about 1 ½'' apart at slightly different angles.
2. Cover 2 more blocks with icing and set them at angles on the first 3.
3. Cover the last block with icing and set it on top.
4. Add trimming around the edges of the blocks, numbers

and letters on the blocks, and a border around the edge
of the cardboard with Royal Icing and a decorator's tube.

Freight Train

Depending upon what you choose for "freight"—small kitchen utensils, nursery items, or candy—a cookie freight train makes an appropriate centerpiece for almost any kind of party including a bridal shower, baby shower, or child's birthday party. You can also wrap a toy-filled train with cellophane and present it to a child on Christmas or some other special occasion.

Although the instructions here call for coconut bars, you can easily substitute graham crackers, which are more nutritious and also more easily available. Just cut them into the approximate size of coconut bars (1 5/8″ x 2 3/8″) and proceed with the directions below.

Materials needed for an engine and 6 cars:
1 package coconut bars
10 scalloped buttercup cookies 2″ in diameter
1 double graham cracker or equivalent quantity of thin sugar wafers
thin rope licorice (approximately 60″)
2 small gumdrops for bell and light
assorted candies for smokestack, windows, and other decoration
Royal Icing (p. 15)
60 Life Savers (5 packages) for wheels; buy extra ones for smokestack if you desire
plywood or heavy cardboard
appropriate tools for cutting plywood or cardboard
aluminum foil
tape

yardstick or ruler
dull knife (for spreading icing)
serrated knife (for cutting cookies)
cutting board
straight pins
decorator's tube (optional)

Wheels

Using Royal Icing, glue 60 Life Savers together in pairs to make 30 double-thickness wheels. (The double thickness is necessary to support the weight of the cars.) Since you must apply the wheels very quickly later on, make them now so that they will dry.

Railroad ties

Like the wheels, the railroad ties must be applied very quickly later on, so make them now. Cut a double graham cracker or thin sugar wafers into 20 pieces (you may not need all of them) measuring approximately $3/8''$ x 1 $1/4''$. If you are using graham crackers, follow the marks where they have been scored by the manufacturer for ease in cutting. If you are using frosting-filled sugar wafers, use only 1 thickness.

Base

1. Measure and cut a piece of plywood or heavy cardboard $6''$ x $24''$. The width allows you to swerve your track slightly for a more pleasing effect, and the length will accommodate a train with an engine and 6 cars. If you wish to add or subtract cars, make your base $3''$ longer or shorter for each car.
2. Cover the board with aluminum foil and tape the foil on the bottom to prevent slipping.
3. Spread a layer of Royal Icing on the top and sides of the

106

foil-covered base. While icing is still wet, move quickly on to the next procedures.

Track

1. Make a track for the train with 2 lengths of thin rope licorice set parallel about 1 ½'' apart. Curve the track on the board so the finished train will not look too stiff. Save extra rope licorice for bell rope which you will attach later.
2. Set graham cracker railroad ties connecting the 2 rails of the track about 1 ⅛'' apart all along the length. You will need 18-20 ties, depending upon how widely you swerve your track. The track in the photograph uses 19 ties.

Setting wheels on the track

While the icing is still moist, place the wheels on the track between the railroad ties. Leave 2 spaces free at the beginning and then set 2 double-thickness wheels between each tie, placing them inside the rails but as close to them as possible. As the icing hardens, the wheels will be secured in position on their rims.

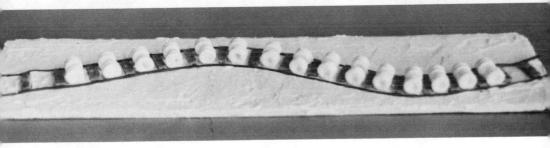

Tinting Royal Icing

Now is the time to tint the rest of the icing to match the coconut bars, if you so desire. By using icing approximately the same color as the cookies, you eliminate the need to hide your seams with decorative trim like the icing you see around the train cars in the photograph.

Designing your train

Decide now how many freight cars you want with high sides and how many with low sides. The train in the photograph consists of 1 engine, 1 caboose, 3 high-sided freight cars, and 2 low-sided freight cars. You may vary this pattern as you wish; however you will need a low freight car for the engineer's cab, so make 1 more than you plan to use otherwise.

Figure 1   Figure 2

Low freight car

1. You will need 3 coconut bars for each low freight car. Set 1 on a work table with the flat side up. This is the bottom of the low-sided freight car.

2. Set another coconut bar on a cutting board with the flat side down. Using a serrated knife and a gentle sawing motion, cut the cookie in half lengthwise. You now have two of the four sides you need for the car (see Figure 1).

3. Spread icing along the raw edges of the cookie halves you have just cut (see Figure 2) and glue the two sides of

the freight car on top of the long edges of the bottom piece. The furrowed sides of the cookie pieces should face outward for a finished appearance (see Figure 3).

Figure 3

4. Set another coconut bar on the cutting board with the flat side down, and cut it in half lengthwise. You will need only 1 of these half pieces.
5. Take 1 half-piece and cut it in half through the width to make 2 quarter pieces.
6. Trim the remaining round side off each quarter piece. You should now have 2 cookie pieces with raw, flat edges on the bottoms and sides but round edges on the tops (see Figure 4).

Figure 4

7. Test each of the 2 cookie pieces for size by fitting them in place at the ends of the freight car. If they don't fit smoothly between the two sides already in place, trim them again with your knife.
8. Spread Royal Icing on the three raw edges of each small cookie piece and glue them in position at the ends of the low freight car (see Figure 5).

Figure 5

High freight car

1. You will need 4 coconut bars for each high freight car. Set 1 on a work table with the flat side up. This is the bottom of the high freight car.
2. Take 2 more coconut bars and cut one rounded edge from each along the length. Do not trim away any more of each cookie than is necessary to give you a flat edge for gluing (see Figure 6).
3. Spread Royal Icing along the raw edges of the cookies you have just cut and glue them in place on top of the long edges of the bottom piece for sides of the high

110

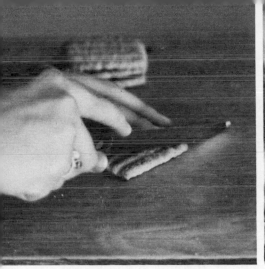

Figure 6   Figure 7

freight car. The furrowed sides of the upright cookies should face outward (see Figure 7).

4. Take another coconut bar and cut it in half through the width.
5. Trim the remaining round side and the round bottom off each half piece. You should now have 2 cookie pieces with raw, flat edges on the bottom and two sides but a round edge at the top.
6. Test both of the 2 cookie pieces for size by fitting them in place at the ends of the freight car. If they don't fit smoothly between the two sides already in position, trim them again with your knife.
7. Spread Royal Icing on the three raw edges of each cookie piece and glue them in place at the ends of the high freight car (see Figure 8).

Figure 8

Engine

1. Set 1 low freight car aside to use later as the engineer's cab.
2. Using Royal Icing, glue 10 buttercup cookies on top of each other for the front of the engine. Keep the scallops as even as possible and use only a tiny amount of icing so it won't spread to the outside edges, where it will show. You may want to let the frosting fill up the hole in the middle at least partially, however. This will keep the gumdrop light from falling down through the hole (see Figure 9).

Figure 9   Figure 10

LIGHT

Glue a small gumdrop in the hole on the top of the stack of cookies for the light on the engine. Keep the cookies in an upright stack until nearly dry (see Figure 10).

SUPPORT FOR ENGINE

Turn the stack of buttercup cookies on its side and glue it to the flat side of a coconut bar. This is the front of the engine (see Figure 11).

Figure 11	Figure 12

ENGINEER'S CAB

1. Take a low freight car and turn it on end. Set it next to the front of the engine to compare their height. You may wish to elevate the cab farther by gluing a half coconut bar (cut through the width) to the bottom of the cab.
2. Using Royal Icing, glue the front of the engine to the engineer's cab so that the hollow side of the cab will face the next car on the train (see Figure 12).

BELL

Glue a small gumdrop on the top of the engine about 1'' from the cab for a bell.

WINDOWS

Make windows for the cab with small candies or with icing from a decorating tube.

113

Glue a cylindrical candy (such as a short length of stick candy) to the front of the engine for a smokestack. If you prefer, you can glue 4 or 5 Life Savers on top of each other for a smokestack. (A small birthday candle inside the Life Savers is an appropriate addition if the train is to be used for a child's birthday.)

BELL ROPE

1. Cut a length of thin rope licorice about 7″ long.
2. Using straight pins, attach one end of the licorice to the bell and the other end of the licorice to a window on the engineer's cab (see Figure 13).

Figure 13

1. Place a dab of Royal Icing on each of the first 6 wheels already attached to the track.
2. Set the engine in position on the 6 wheels so that the front of the engine rests on 4 wheels and the cab of the engine rests on 2 wheels.

Cattle catcher
1. Cut 1 coconut bar in half through the width and spread Royal Icing along the raw edge.
2. Lean the cattle catcher from the track to the front of the engine below the light at a slight angle.

Caboose

BOTTOM

You will need 5 coconut bars for the caboose. Set 1 on a work table with the flat side up. This is the bottom of the caboose.

BACK
1. Trim the rounded edges from two short ends of another coconut bar.
2. Spread Royal Icing on one raw edge you have just cut and glue the back of the caboose upright at one end of the bottom, furrowed side out.

SIDES
1. Cut 1 coconut bar in half lengthwise.
2. Trim the round short edges on both sides of each cookie half. You should now have 2 cookie pieces which have flat raw edges on three sides but a round edge along one length (see Figure 14).
3. Spread Royal Icing on one short end and the long raw side of each cookie half and glue both of them upright

Figure 14   Figure 15

against the back of the caboose, furrowed sides out (see Figure 15).

FRONT

Cut a coconut bar in half through the width. Set 1 half aside for the railing and glue the other half in place as the front of the caboose. This will leave the upper part of the caboose exposed for a window (see Figure 16).

RAILING

1. Cut the half coconut bar in half again to make a narrow railing the width of the caboose (see Figure 17).

Figure 16   Figure 17

2. Glue the railing in place on the far edge of the caboose platform.

ROOF

Spread Royal Icing along the top of the back and side pieces of the caboose and glue 1 whole coconut bar on top, furrowed side up (see Figure 18). Line it up evenly with the bottom of the caboose but approximately 2 1/4" above it (see Figure 19).

Figure 18   Figure 19

Decorating the train
Add decorative icing along the seams of the train cars as desired, including the engine. All decoration should be completely dry before you proceed.

Attaching the cars
1. Decide now if you want your cars permanently attached to the track. (You have already attached the engine to the track because the cattle catcher on the engine will pose

117

problems if it and the engine are not firmly mounted in place.) The advantage of *not* securing the remaining cars to the track is that you can give them away as individual party favors if you wish.

2. Should you decide to attach the cars, follow this procedure. Put a dab of Royal Icing glue on the top of each of the first four wheels behind the engine. Gently set a freight car on the wheels, keeping the car as parallel as possible to the train rails beneath it. Add the other cars in order.

Caution: Remove straight pins if the train is to be eaten.

Spring Bonnet

Would-be milliners can let themselves go decorating dainty cookie bonnets. What's more, the results are good enough to eat.

Materials needed for each bonnet:
1 small (1 ¾'') marshmallow cookie trimmed with pastel frosting
1 round vanilla cookie measuring 2 ½'' in diameter
Royal Icing (p. 15) Tint in a variety of pastel shades.
decorator's tube
dull knife (for spreading icing)
additional wire, paper, scissors, candies, as desired

Assembly
Spread Royal Icing on the bottom of a marshmallow cookie and glue on the top center of a vanilla cookie.

Decoration
1. Add ribbons, ruffles, bows, flowers with icing from a decorator's tube.
2. Add additional decoration with paper, wire, and candies, as desired.

Mortar Board

So easy they can be made at the last minute, these miniature mortar boards will give special meaning to a graduation day party. The chocolate on the cookies melts easily, however, so be careful where you set them in warm weather.

Materials needed for each mortar board:
1 square (not oblong) chocolate covered graham cracker
1 chocolate poppins cookie 1 1/2'' in diameter or chocolate marshmallow cookie
1 small round candy (optional)
Royal Icing (p. 15) Add dry cocoa to make it brown.
thin rope licorice 2 1/4'' long
dull knife (for spreading icing)
scissors
decorator's tube (optional)

Assembly
1. Set the chocolate poppins cookie on a work table. This is the crown of the hat.
2. Attach the chocolate covered graham cracker squarely on top, using Royal Icing.
3. With clean scissors cut a piece of thin rope licorice 2 1/4'' long.
4. Glue one end of the licorice to the center top of the graham cracker so that the other end falls over the side like a tassle.
5. Attach a small candy in the center top of the hat or swirl a small bit of icing from a decorator's tube.

Christmas Tree

A cookie Christmas tree adorned with sugar cube "gifts" lends old-fashioned charm to a holiday table. You can make a forest of trees of different shapes—short and fat to tall and skinny—by changing the height but not the size of the base of the 4 isosceles triangles that form the structure.

Unfortunately, peanut creme cookies are highly susceptible to humidity, and this design is not recommended for humid climates. See *Effects of Humidity*, p. 18.

Materials needed for each 8" tree:
4 peanut creme cookies (1 1/3" packages)
20-24 sugar cubes, assorted sizes
1/3 cup small candies, such as red and white candy sticks
     broken in chunks (optional)
Royal Icing (p. 15) Tint bright red and bright green.
serrated knife (for cutting cookies)
dull knife (for spreading icing)
ruler
decorator's tube
cutting board
string, wire, or rubber bands

Sides
1. Set a peanut creme cookie flat side down on a cutting board.
2. With a tip of a sharp knife mark the center of the cookie 8" from one end. This marks the top of the tree.
3. Set your ruler from the mark on the cookie to the corner

edge 8'' away, and cut very gently with a sawing motion, using the straight edge of the ruler to guide your knife.

4. Repeat step 3 from the mark at the center to the other corner edge of the cookie to make an isosceles triangle 8'' high.

5. Repeat steps 1-4 to make three more sides for the tree.

6. Note that each peanut creme cookie is a sandwich composed of 1 flat cookie, 1 bulky cookie, and a peanut butter filling. Using your ruler and serrated knife, cut away ⅜'' along both long sides of each bulky cookie so you can glue the 4 triangles together in a pyramid structure. Also remove any exposed peanut butter, which will not adhere well to Royal Icing.

Assembly

1. Spread the two long sides of each triangle with Royal Icing, and glue the 4 triangles into a pyramid.

2. Hold the structure together with string, wire, or rubber bands until the icing dries completely—several hours to overnight.

Decoration

1. Remove string, wire, and rubber bands before proceeding.
2. Using bright red and green icing and a decorator's tube, draw lines on each sugar cube to represent ribbons on gift packages. Let dry.
3. Decorate 1 triangle of the Christmas tree at a time by swirling green Royal Icing from the base toward the point and apply sugar cubes and candy pieces to the moist icing as you work. Decorate all 4 triangles and let dry.
4. Apply a swirl of icing to the top of the tree for a star (optional).

Baseball Cap

These simple cookie caps can be decorated to resemble baseball caps, train engineers' caps, or even firemen's hats.

Materials needed for each baseball cap:
1 thin chocolate wafer measuring 2 ¼'' in diameter
1 chocolate poppins cookie 1 ½'' in diameter or chocolate marshmallow cookie
1 small candy such as M & M or Hersheyette
Royal Icing (p. 15) Tint as desired.
dull knife (for spreading icing)
decorator's tube

Brim
Set the chocolate wafer on a work table.

Crown
Spread Royal Icing on the bottom of the poppins cookie and glue it near one edge of the wafer. Let dry.

Decoration
1. With Royal Icing and a decorator's tube draw thin lines up the grooves of the poppins cookie from the brim to the top.
2. Draw team letters on each cap as desired.
3. Glue a small candy in the top of the cap to hide the hole.

Turtle

If you've never seen a turtle move fast, watch how quickly guests will snatch these charming cookie creatures.

Materials needed for each turtle:
1 2'' scalloped buttercup cookie
1 chocolate marshmallow cookie measuring 1¾'' in diameter
5 almonds
thin rope licorice ¾'' long
Royal Icing (p. 15)
dull knife (for spreading icing)
sharp knife (for cutting almonds)
scissors
decorator's tube

Assembly
Spread Royal Icing on bottom of marshmallow cookie and glue it top center to the scalloped cookie.

Shell
With white icing and a decorator's tube, draw scallops on marshmallow cookie to resemble turtle's shell.

Head
1. Insert 1 whole almond in end of marshmallow cookie for head.
2. Make 2 dots of icing on head with decorator's tube for eyes.

Feet

1. Cut round ends from 4 almonds.
2. Glue cut ends of almonds to marshmallow cookie to resemble feet.

Tail

1. Insert end of licorice into marshmallow cookie for tail.
2. Cut exposed end of tail into a point with scissors.

Big-game hunters can capture this friendly lion without resistance to take home a trophy. He's made from 5 cookies in various shapes and sizes.

Materials needed for each lion:
1 scalloped sugar ring cookie 3″ in diameter
1 chocolate marshmallow cookie 1 3/4″ in diameter
1 chocolate marshmallow cookie 2″ in diameter (or larger)
2 round cookies at least 2″ in diameter
thin rope licorice—approximately 5″
4 almonds
2 small gumdrops
Royal Icing (p. 15) Tint light brown, dark brown, and other
   colors as desired.
serrated knife (for cutting cookies)
cutting board
dull knife (for spreading icing)
decorator's tube

Head
Remove hard cookie from base of small marshmallow cookie. With Royal Icing, glue remaining marshmallow to center top of scalloped cookie for face and mane of lion. Let dry.

Body
1. Trim 2 round cookies to match the size of the large marshmallow cookie at the base.
2. Glue the 2 round cookies under the marshmallow cookie to give it height.

Assembly

1. Spread light brown frosting over entire surface of lion's body and while icing is still moist attach the head and mane in position tilting slightly back and resting at one edge on the work table.
2. Cut the round ends from 4 almonds and insert into larger marshmallow cookie for feet.
3. Insert the rope licorice at back for a tail.
4. Trim 2 gumdrops as necessary and attach them to top of head for ears.

Decoration

With decorator's tube and Royal Icing, add eyes, nose, mouth, and curlicues for mane.

Safari Hat

Proper attire for a party safari calls for a hat made from 2 light tan cookies.

Materials needed for 1 hat:
1 pastel-colored marshmallow cookie measuring 1 ¾'' in diameter
1 round sugar cookie measuring 2 ¾'' in diameter
Royal Icing (p. 15) Tint part of it brown.
dull knife (for spreading icing)
decorator's tube

Assembly
Using Royal Icing, attach marshmallow cookie to center top of sugar cookie.

Decoration
1. With brown icing and a decorator's tube, draw 8 lines on the crown of the hat from the brim to the top.
2. Make a small button on top with a swirl of brown icing.

Circus Train

A captivating centerpiece for a children's party, this circus train can be displayed by itself or with the circus tent which follows.

Materials needed for an engine, calliope, and 4 animal cars:

1 package coconut bars
10 scalloped buttercup cookies 2″ in diameter
1 double graham cracker or equivalent quantity of thin sugar wafers
thin rope licorice (approximately 60″)
2 small gumdrops for bell and light.
52 Life Savers (5 packages) for wheels; use extra ones for smokestack, if you desire
assorted candies for smokestack and other decoration
Royal Icing (p. 15) Tint as desired.
50 pretzel sticks at least 2″ long
4 animal crackers
1 small pastel-colored marshmallow cookie 1 ¾″ in diameter (Select a brand of cookie which is firm rather than soft, or allow cookie to get slightly stale.)
plywood or heavy cardboard
appropriate tools for cutting plywood or cardboard
aluminum foil
tape
yardstick or ruler
dull knife (for spreading icing)
serrated knife (for cutting cookies)

cutting board
straight pins
decorator's tube
ice pick or metal skewer

Wheels

Using Royal Icing, glue 52 Life Savers together in pairs to make 26 double-thickness wheels. (The double thickness is necessary to support the weight of the cars.) Since you must apply the wheels very quickly later on, make them now and let them be drying.

Railroad ties

Like the wheels, the railroad ties must be applied very quickly later on, so make them now. Cut a double graham cracker or thin sugar wafers into 18 pieces (you may not need all of them) measuring approximately ⅜" x 1 ¼". If you are using graham crackers, follow the marks where they have been scored by the manufacturer for ease in cutting. If you are using frosting-filled sugar wafers, use only 1 thickness.

Base

1. Measure and cut a piece of plywood or heavy cardboard 6" x 21". The width allows you to swerve your track slightly for a more pleasing effect, and the length will accommodate a train with an engine and 5 cars (1 calliope and 4 animal cars). If you wish to add or subtract cars, make your base 3" longer or shorter for each car.
2. Cover the board with aluminum foil and tape the foil on the bottom to prevent slipping.
3. Spread a layer of Royal Icing on the top and sides of the foil-covered base. While icing is still moist, move quickly on to the next procedures.

Track

1. Consult the photographs accompanying the Freight Train (p. 105), remembering that the instructions for the circus train call for an engine and 5 cars while the instructions for the freight train call for an engine and 6 cars. (The freight train therefore has a longer track and uses more wheels.)
2. Make a track for the train with 2 lengths of thin rope licorice set parallel about 1 1/2'' apart. Curve the track on the board so the finished train will not look too stiff. Save extra rope licorice for bell rope which you will attach later.
3. Set graham cracker (or sugar wafer) railroad ties connecting the 2 rails of the track about 1 1/8'' apart all along the length. You will need 16-18 ties, depending upon how widely you swerve your track. The track in the photograph uses 19 ties for an engine and 6 cars.

Setting wheels on the track

While icing is still moist, place the wheels on the track between the railroad ties. Leave 2 spaces free at the beginning and then set 2 double-thickness wheels between each tie, placing them inside the rails but as close to them as possible. As the icing hardens, the wheels will be secured in position on their rims.

Engine

CAB (See pictures for low freight car, p. 108.)

1. You will need 3 coconut bars for the cab, which you make as a horizontal structure and then turn on end after it has dried. Set 1 bar on a work table with the flat side up.
2. Set another coconut bar on a cutting board with the flat

133

side down. Using a serrated knife and a gentle sawing motion, cut the cookie in half lengthwise.

3. Spread icing along the raw edges of the cookie halves you have just cut and glue them upright on top of the long edges of the whole cookie, furrowed sides facing outward.

4. Set another coconut bar on the cutting board with the flat side down and cut it in half lengthwise. You will need only 1 of these half pieces.

5. Take 1 half-piece and cut it in half through the width to make 2 quarter-pieces.

6. Trim the remaining round side (but not the round top) off each quarter piece.

7. Test each of the 2 quarter-pieces you have just cut to see if they are the right size to fit as ends in the horizontal structure you are making. If they don't fit smoothly, trim them again with your knife.

8. Spread Royal Icing on the 3 raw edges of each cookie piece and glue it in position at an end.

FRONT

Using Royal Icing, glue 10 scalloped buttercup cookies on top of each other. Keep the scallops as even as possible and use only a tiny amount of icing so it won't spread to the outside edges, where it will show. You may want to let the frosting fill up the hole in the middle at least partially, however. This will keep the gumdrop light from falling down through the hole.

LIGHT

Glue a small gumdrop in the hole on the top of the stack of cookies for the light on the engine. Keep the cookies in an upright stack until nearly dry.

SUPPORT

Turn the stack of buttercup cookies on its side and glue it to the flat side of a coconut bar.

ASSEMBLY

1. Take the horizontal structure you have made for the engineer's cab and turn it on end. Set it next to the front of the engine to compare their height. You may wish to elevate the cab farther by gluing a half coconut bar (cut through the width) to the bottom of the cab.
2. Using Royal Icing, glue the front of the engine to the engineer's cab so that the hollow side of the cab will face the next car on the train.

BELL

Glue a small gumdrop on the top of the engine about 1″ from the cab for a bell.

WINDOWS

Make windows for the cab with small candies or with icing from a decorator's tube.

SMOKESTACK

Make a smokestack with 1 cylindrical candy or several Life Savers glued together. (A small birthday candle inside the Life Savers is an appropriate addition if the train is to be used for a child's birthday.)

BELL ROPE

1. Cut a length of thin rope licorice about 7″ long.
2. Using straight pins, attach one end of the licorice to the bell and the other end to a window on the engineer's cab.

ATTACHING THE ENGINE TO THE TRACK

1. Place a dab of Royal Icing on each of the first 6 wheels already attached to the track.

2. Set the engine in position on 4 double-thickness wheels, or, if you feel it needs more support, on 6 wheels so that the front of the engine rests on 4 double-thickness wheels and the cab of the engine rests on 2 double-thickness wheels.

Cattle catcher
1. Cut 1 coconut bar in half through the width and spread Royal Icing along the raw edge.
2. Lean the cattle catcher from the track to the front of the engine below the light at a slight angle. (see p. 118, for picture of Freight Train with attached cattle catcher.)

Calliope

FLOOR REST

Set 1 whole coconut bar on a work table, flat side up.

PIPE REST
1. Cut another coconut bar in half lengthwise (see Figure 1).
2. Glue the 2 halves of the coconut bar together one on top of another to make a half-size double-thickness cookie.
3. Spread the raw edge of the double-thickness cookie with icing and glue it upright on top of the far side of the coconut bar floor.

KEYBOARD
1. Cut a piece from another coconut bar the full length and $1/4$ the width.
2. Spread icing along the raw edge of this long cookie piece and attach the cookie to the floor so it is flush against the pipe rest on the edge. When you are through constructing the calliope, you will draw a keyboard on the top

Figure 1   Figure 2

surface of this long narrow cookie with icing and a decorator's tube.

LOWER PIPES

1. Cut a marshmallow cookie in half. You will need only 1 of these 2 pieces (see Figure 2).
2. Glue the cut side of the cookie half on top of the double-thickness cookie so that the flat edge faces the keyboard. When you are through constructing the calliope, you will draw pipes on the flat side of the marshmallow cookie with a decorator's tube and Royal Icing.

UPPER PIPES

1. Cut 5-7 pretzels to measure 2" long.
2. Make upper pipes for the calliope by inserting the pretzels into the marshmallow cookie so they fan out from the rim of the half circle (see Figure 3).

DECORATION

Using Royal Icing and a decorator's tube, draw keys on the keyboard, lower pipes on the marshmallow cookie, and

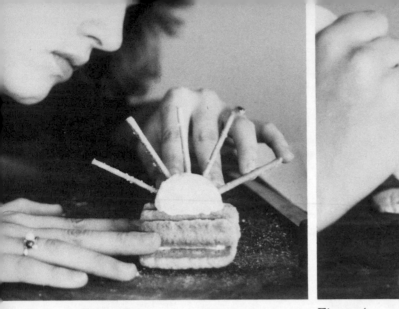

Figure 3   Figure 4

other ornate designs as desired to resemble the trimming on an elaborate calliope.

Animal car

FLOOR OF CAGE

1. Set 1 coconut bar on the work table with furrowed side up. This is the floor of the cage (see Figure 4).
2. Glue 1 animal cracker upright on the cookie floor with Royal Icing, taking advantage of a groove in the cookie to help hold the animal vertical.

BARS OF CAGE

1. Cut 10 pretzel sticks as evenly as possible into 2'' lengths.
2. With your decorator's tube run a border of icing around the top edge of the floor.
3. Stick 10 pretzels upright in the icing, 4 on each side, 1 on each end. Set them as evenly and as straight as possible. While frosting is still moist, move quickly to next procedures (see Figure 5, Figure 6).

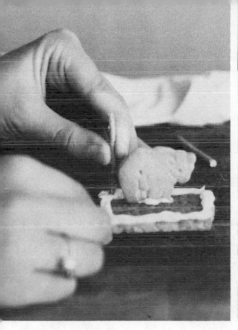

Figure 5   Figure 6

ROOF OF CAGE

1. Take another coconut bar and run a border of icing from a decorator's tube around the edge of the flat surface of the cookie (see Figure 7).

2. Set the roof on top of the upright pretzel sticks so that the pretzels will stick in the icing border you have just drawn. Straighten pretzels as necessary and let dry (see Figure 8).

Figure 7   Figure 8

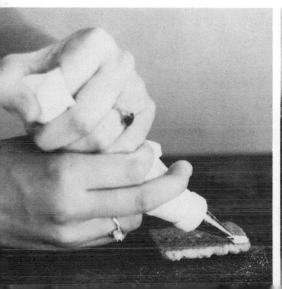

Attaching cars to each other (optional)

1. With an ice pick or metal skewer drill a hole in each end of the floor of the calliope and every animal cage. Also drill a hole at the back of the engineer's cabin on the floor.
2. Cut pretzel sticks into lengths approximately 1 1/4'' long.
3. As you set each car on the track, attach it also to the car in front of it by means of a pretzel stick inserted into the holes you have just drilled. Use icing as necessary to hold pretzels in place (see Figure 9).

Attaching cars to track

1. Spread Royal Icing on the tops of the 4 double Life Saver wheels behind the engine, and set the calliope in place.
2. Add other cars in turn.

Decoration

Add trimming as desired with small candies and icing from a decorator's tube.

Caution: Remove straight pins if the train is to be eaten.

Circus Tent and Performing Animals

A circus spells excitement for young or old. Brighten your party table with a pile of balloons and a gay circus tent made from peanut creme cookies. Performing animals mounted on marshmallow cookies add to the fun.

Unfortunately, peanut creme cookies are highly susceptible to humidity, and this design is not recommended for humid climates. See *Effects of Humidity*, p. 18.

CIRCUS TENT

Materials needed for 1 circus tent:
6 long peanut creme cookies (2 packages)
3-5 flat-bottomed, edible ice cream cups
1-2 sugar cubes
Royal Icing (p. 15) Tint in a variety of colors.
bright ribbon approximately 1″ wide and 2 ½″ long
glue
scissors
regular 6″ pipe cleaner
round tray, or dish, or cardboard, etc. at least 8 ½″ in
　　diameter on which to mount tent
ruler
serrated knife (for cutting cookies)
dull knife (for spreading icing)
cutting board
decorator's tube
string

Sides

1. Set each cookie on a cutting board with the flat side down. Using a gentle sawing motion and the straight edge of the ruler to guide your knife, cut a length from

each cookie measuring 4 1/4''. These 6 pieces will form the sides of the tent.

2. Notice that each peanut creme cookie is a sandwich composed of 1 flat cookie, 1 bulky cookie, and a peanut butter filling. The bulky cookie and the peanut butter filling will cause problems when you try to glue the sides of the tent together, so cut them away in a border 3/8'' wide on each cookie side (but not on the top or bottom).

3. Spread Royal Icing along the sides of the 6 cookies and glue them into a hexagon 4 1/4'' tall mounted on a tray, dish, wooden board, or piece of heavy cardboard.

4. Tie the hexagon with string as needed to hold it in position until the icing dries.

5. Remove string and proceed.

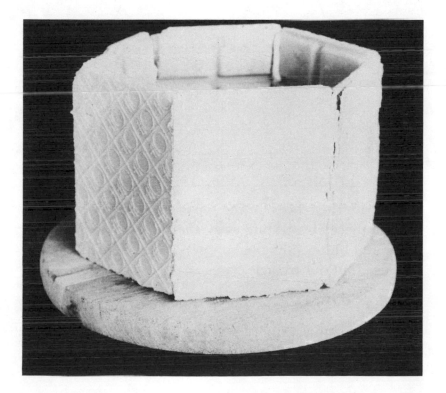

Top pieces

1. From each remaining cookie piece cut an isosceles triangle the width of the cookie 4 ½'' high. These 6 triangles will form the top of the tent.

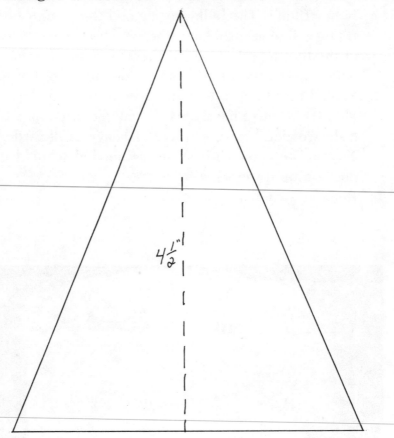

$4\frac{1}{2}''$

2. Prepare the pieces for the top of the tent as you did the side pieces by cutting away the bulky cookie and the peanut butter filling in borders ⅜'' wide on all triangle sides (but not triangle bases).

Support

1. Make a center support piece by stacking flat-bottomed ice cream cups upside-down (and whole or partial sugar

cubes, as needed) to a height of about 6 ¼″. The exact height depends on several factors, so test your support to see if the triangles rest upon it properly before gluing them together.

2. Spread Royal Icing along the sides and bottoms of the 6 triangles and glue them together in a peak at the top of the tent. Let dry.

Flag
1. Glue a ribbon approximately 1″ wide and 2 ½″ long to a 6″ pipe cleaner for a flag.
2. Insert the pipe cleaner into the top of the tent.

Decoration
Decorate the tent as desired with bright-colored icing.

PERFORMING ANIMALS

Performing circus animals are so easy to assemble and add such a lively touch to a circus party that you'll want to make dozens. If humidity rules out a circus tent as a centerpiece, you can use these animals as party favors in conjunction with the Circus Train (p. 131).

Materials needed for 1 performing animal:
1 animal cracker
1 marshmallow cookie 1 3/4'' in diameter
1 round flat cookie 2 1/2'' in diameter
Royal Icing (p. 15) Tint in several shades.
dull knife (for spreading icing)
decorator's tube

Assembly
Spread the bottom of a marshmallow cookie with Royal Icing and glue to the center top of a round flat cookie.

Mounting animal
1. Run a strip of icing from a decorator's tube about 1'' on the top of the marshmallow cookie.
2. Set an animal cracker upright in the icing.

Decoration
Cover the seam where the two cookies join with 1 or more bands of icing from a decorator's tube.

Pilgrim and Indian

A cookie Pilgrim and Indian can team up for a Thanksgiving table. Or use the Indian alone for a child's birthday party.

Materials needed for 1 Pilgrim:
1 flat-bottomed, edible ice cream cup measuring 1 1/4'' at the base
2 pastel-colored marshmallow cookies 1 3/4'' in diameter
1 plain round cookie 3'' in diameter
Royal Icing (p. 15) Tint in several shades.
dull knife (for spreading icing)
decorator's tube

Head
1. The fullness of marshmallow cookies varies from manufacturer to manufacturer. Hold the flat sides of the 2 marshmallow cookies together and study the shape to see if you should remove 1 or both of the hard cookies under the marshmallows.
2. Remove the hard cookies as necessary and glue the flat sides of the marshmallows together with Royal Icing to form a round head.

Collar
Glue the head on a plain round cookie with the seam down so you have a round surface (without a seam) for the face. The supporting cookie will serve as the collar.

Hair
Make hair for Pilgrim with brown icing and decorator's tube, covering the seam where you have joined the 2 marshmallow cookies. Attach hat while icing is still moist.

Hat

Break ice cream cup piece by piece until you come to the line about 2'' from the bottom. Place the cup upside down on the Pilgrim's head for a hat.

Decoration

Add eyes, nose, mouth, hat band, and outline for collar with icing and a decorator's tube.

Materials needed for 1 Indian:

2 chocolate marshmallow cookies 1 ¾'' at the base
1 plain round cookie 3'' in diameter
Royal Icing (p. 15) Use black and several other shades.
dull knife (for spreading icing)
decorator's tube

Head

1. The fullness of marshmallow cookies varies from brand to brand. Hold the 2 marshmallow cookies you are using so their flat sides are together and study the shape to see if you should remove 1 or both of the hard cookies supporting the marshmallows.
2. Remove the hard cookies as necessary and glue the flat sides of the marshmallows together with Royal Icing to form a round head.

Support

Glue the head on a plain round cookie with the seam down so you have a round surface (without a seam) for the face.

Hair

Make hair for the Indian with black icing and a decorator's tube, covering the seam at the side where you have joined the 2 marshmallow cookies.

Decoration

Make a head band, eyes, nose, mouth, and other decorations as desired with colored icing and a decorator's tube.

Drum

Brightly decorated drums make suitable favors at an Indian party for small children or a record party for teenagers.

Materials needed for set of 3 drums:
5 vanilla wafers measuring 1 ½'' in diameter
3 round sugar cookies measuring 3'' in diameter
4 chocolate wafers measuring 2 ¼'' in diameter
Royal Icing (p. 15) Leave some white and tint the rest in
  several shades.
dull knife (for spreading icing)
decorator's tube

Assembly
Using Royal Icing, glue the 3 kinds of cookies into 3 different stacks.

Decoration
1. Frost tops white.
2. Frost sides with desired colors, being careful to fill in all grooves. Let dry.
3. Add zigzags of contrasting icing around sides with a decorator's tube.
4. Make contrasting borders around tops with a decorator's tube.

Banjo

Hummers and strummers will appreciate this novel party favor—a banjo made from graham crackers and round cookies.

Materials needed for each banjo:
3 chocolate wafers 2 ½'' in diameter and ¼'' thick
1 double graham cracker
Royal Icing (p. 15) Tint in two or more shades; keep some
   white.
dull knife (for spreading icing)
serrated knife (for cutting crackers)
cutting board
ruler
decorator's tube

Assembly
1. Glue chocolate wafers together with Royal Icing.
2. Frost top white.
3. Cut 2 lengthwise strips off double graham cracker about ⅝'' wide.
4. Glue graham cracker strips together one on top of another and let dry.
5. Trim about ½'' off length of graham crackers and glue to the side of the stack of round cookies.
6. Frost everything except top with colored frosting and let dry.
7. Decorate the border of the round top with icing from a tube.
8. Put icing "strings" down the neck of the banjo.

Xylophone

Peanut creme cookies and graham crackers combine for a musical treat.

Materials needed for 1 xylophone:
2 peanut creme cookies (2/3 package)
2 double graham crackers
2 candy sticks about 5'' long and ½'' in diameter
2 candy balls about 1'' in diameter
Royal Icing (p. 15) Tint some tan, the rest in bright shades.
dull knife (for spreading icing)
serrated knife (for cutting cookies)
cutting board
ruler
decorator's tube

Sides
Set 1 peanut creme cookie on a cutting board flat side down and cut in half lengthwise. These 2 pieces are the sides.

Wide end
1. Set another peanut creme cookie on a cutting board and cut in half lengthwise. You will use only one of these halves.
2. From 1 long, narrow cookie cut a piece 3 sections long. This is the wide end of the xylophone.

Narrow end
From a long, narrow cookie cut a piece 1 ½ sections long.

Assembly

Trim the bulky edges of the cookie as necessary and glue the 4 cookie pieces together with tan Royal Icing, flat side out. Let dry.

Keys

1. From 2 double graham crackers cut 6 pieces 5/8'' wide and the full length of the double cracker. Saw them very carefully so crackers won't break where they have been scored.
2. From these strips cut 6 "keys" the proper length to span the inner, bulky cookie of the xylophone rim but not the outer narrow half of the peanut creme cookie.
3. Set keys about 1/2'' apart and glue in place with tan Royal Icing.

Decoration

1. Decorate top edges and all seams of xylophone with colored icing from a decorator's tube.
2. Run a thin line of frosting around each key and put 2 dots of icing at each end to look like nails.

Mallets

Glue candy balls to ends of candy sticks to make 2 mallets.

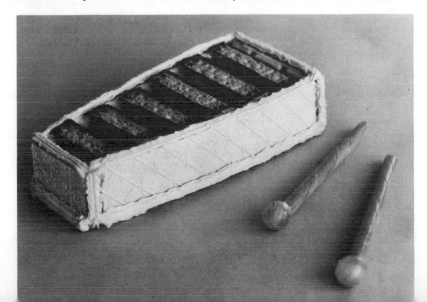

Noah's Ark

Two-by-two the animals march up a long peanut creme ramp to a brightly-decorated ark ready to set sail. This graham cracker boat demonstrates one of hundreds of ways that Bible stories, legends, and myths can be adapted to cookie craft.

Materials needed for 1 ark:
3 peanut creme cookies (1 package)
20 double graham crackers
10 animal crackers (in pairs, 2 of a kind)
Royal Icing (p. 15) Tint some to match graham crackers, the
    rest in two bright shades.
dull knife (for spreading icing)
serrated knife (for cutting crackers and cookies)
cutting board
ruler
decorator's tube

Deck
1. Lay 1 peanut creme cookie flat side down on a cutting board. Cut away a strip 1″ wide along the entire length of the cookie using a gentle sawing motion against the straight edge of your ruler.

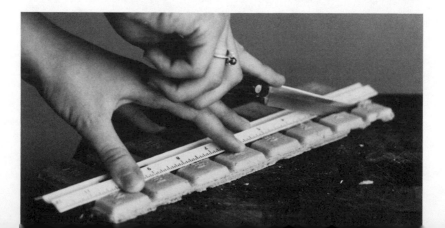

2. Repeat step 1 to remove a 1″ strip from another cookie.
3. With tan Royal Icing, glue the 2 original cookies together along their cut edges to make 1 large cookie measuring approximately 5″ x 10 ¾″. Let dry.
4. Cut away the four corners of the large cookie to make a flat hexagon with measurements as in the diagram below.

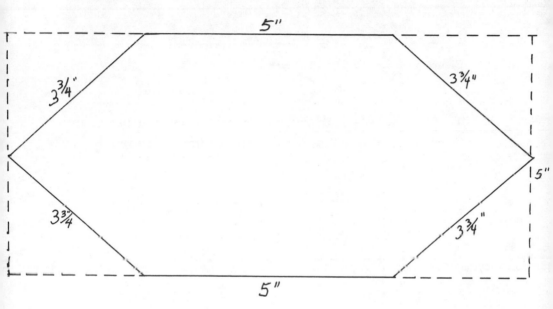

Cabin

FLOOR
1. Glue 2 double graham crackers together, one on top of another, with tan icing. Let dry (see Figure 1).
2. Trim ¼″ from one short end of the double-thickness cracker.
3. Glue the cracker in the center of the deck for the floor of the cabin. This floor will not be seen when the cabin is finished, but it will provide a support for gluing the sides and ends of the cabin in position.

Figure 1   Figure 2

ENDS

1. Set a double graham cracker on the cutting board and gently cut it into a shape as shown in the diagram below (see Figure 2).

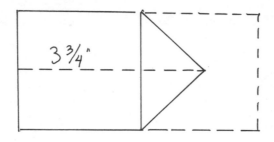

3 ¾ "

2. Repeat step 1 to make the other end for the cabin.
3. Glue the two ends for the cabin upright from the deck and against (not ON) the floor of the cabin (see Figure 3).

SIDES

1. Make a side for the cabin by gluing 1 double graham cracker horizontally. Set it upright from the deck and against (not ON) the cabin floor (see Figure 4).
2. Repeat step 1 to make the other side for the cabin.

Figure 3   Figure 4

ROOF

1. Make a pitched roof for the cabin with 2 double graham
    crackers glued horizontally so that they rest on the peaks
    provided by the ends of the cabin. The roof will slightly
    overhang the sides (see Figure 5).

Figure 5

2. Fill all cracks left in the construction of the cabin with tan Royal Icing.

Railing
1. Glue 12 double graham crackers together in pairs to make 6 double-thickness crackers for the six sides of the deck. Let dry.
2. Bevel 2 railing pieces on both short ends.
3. Glue the 2 beveled railing pieces (beveled sides in) to the two long sides of the deck. Set them outside (not ON) the deck, upright from the working table. Let dry.
4. All the other four sides of the railing must be trimmed as well as beveled. The exact dimensions of the ends you cut away will depend upon several factors, including how carefully to specification you cut the cookie for the deck and what brand of graham crackers you are using. You must therefore hold each railing piece in position to measure how much to trim away. Trim and bevel all railing pieces.
5. Glue the entire railing around the ark and let dry.

Animal ramp
1. Line up 10 animal crackers in 5 pairs.
2. Set 1 peanut creme cookie flat side up on a working table.
3. With colored icing and a decorator's tube, draw 2 strips of frosting the entire length of the cookie about 1 1/4'' apart.
4. Set the animals upright in the frosting to resemble male and female animals marching to the ark in pairs. Let dry.

Decoration
Trim seams and add borders as desired with colored icing from a decorator's tube. Let dry.

Assembly
Set animal ramp so that one end rests on the railing of the ark.

"Haunted" House

A spooky and distinctive centerpiece for a Halloween party is a "haunted" house assembled from graham cracker cubes of various sizes.

Unfortunately, this large structure may cause problems in an excessively humid climate or in a house cooled by an evaporative air conditioner. For safety's sake, make your large graham cracker cubes two or three days in advance and see how they hold up in your climate before proceeding with the entire structure. See *Effects of Humidity*, p. 18.

Materials needed for 1 house:
3 large graham cracker cubes (p. 18)
6 small graham cracker cubes (p. 22)
8 double graham crackers
double recipe Royal Icing (p. 15) Set aside about ½ cup to leave white and tint yellow. Color the rest brown.
4 or 5 chocolate candy bars to cut up as windows
1 cup broken pretzel sticks
tray, wooden board, heavy cardboard, or other sturdy surface at least 12" x 12" (on which to construct house)
dull knife (for spreading icing)
serrated knife (for cutting crackers)
ruler
cutting board
decorator's tube

General Preparations
1. Make a mini graham cracker cube about 1" square from 1 of the double graham crackers, following the instruc-

tions for the small graham cracker cube on p. 22. This is the top for the tower.

2. Glue 2 double graham crackers together, one on top of another, with Royal Icing. This is the lower porch.
3. Cut 4 double graham crackers into the shape illustrated below. These will form the slanting part of the high tower.

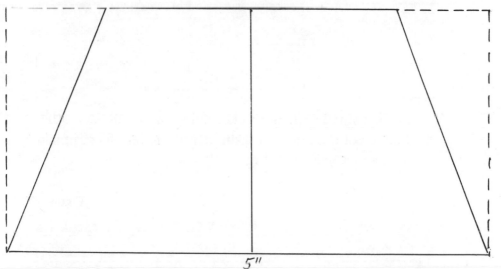

5"

4. Save the remaining double graham cracker to fill up the bare spots on the lower porch.

Assembly

FIRST TWO STORIES OF HOUSE

Set 2 large graham cracker cubes side-by-side on a tray or other sturdy surface. Since each single graham cracker will represent 1 story of the finished house, you now have 2 stories (see Figure 1).

THIRD AND FOURTH STORIES

Set 1 large graham cracker cube slightly off center on top of the other 2. This will add the 3rd and 4th stories of the house and also create 2 porches above the 2nd level (see Figure 2).

Figure 1

TOWERS

1. Stack 4 small graham cracker cubes on top of each other in front of the house and slightly to the left. These make a 4-story tower (see Figure 3).

Figure 2

Figure 3

2. Set 1 small graham cracker cube on the main structure for the main high tower of the house.
3. Set the mini cube on the 4-story tower for a mini tower.

Low porch and entrance
1. Set 1 small cube in front of the house at the far right, leaving a space between it and the tower about 3″ wide for the front entrance.
2. Close in the front entrance and make a porch by setting

the double-thickness graham cracker on the cube at the far right so it extends all the way to the tower at the left.

Final assembly

1. Make a slanting roof for the high tower with the 4 double graham crackers you cut to shape earlier. Set 1 on each of the 4 sides of the 4th story, slanting it from the edge of the house to the tower. Glue the pieces together with Royal Icing as you go (see Figure 4).
2. Fill in the bare spots on the lower porch by cutting graham cracker pieces to size.

Figure 4

Figure 5

Decoration

1. Cover the entire surface of the assembly with brown icing in a thin glossy consistency.
2. While icing is still moist, insert broken pretzel sticks around the edges of the 3 porches for porch railings.
3. Apply chocolate bars cut to shape for windows. Let dry.
4. Add shutters and other decoration as desired with icing from a decorator's tube.

Witch's Hat

A clever party favor to accompany a haunted house center-piece is a witch's hat made from a chocolate wafer and an ice cream cone.

Materials needed for each hat:
1 chocolate wafer 2 3/8'' in diameter
1 ice cream cone
Royal Icing (p. 15) Color black and orange.
dull knife (for spreading icing)
decorator's tube

Assembly
1. Break the rim of the cone away bit by bit until you have a pointed end that will rest at an angle about 3'' high.
2. Mount the cone tip on the center top of the round cookie with Royal Icing.
3. Cover the entire hat with black icing and let dry.
4. Make a band for the hat with orange icing from a decorator's tube.

Pink Castle

For adventurous Camelot fans or avid fairy tale readers, here's a dream castle good enough to eat. You can make it in any size you want because all the units are constructed separately and then assembled together. The castle described here occupies a space approximately 10" x 10" and 15" high, but you adjust the plans to fit your own needs.

Unfortunately, large graham cracker cubes do not hold up well in excessively humid climates or in buildings cooled by evaporative air conditioners. For safety's sake, make your large graham cracker cube two or three days in advance to see if it retains its shape before proceeding with the entire structure. See *Effects of Humidity*, p. 18.

Materials needed for 1 castle:
17 flat-bottomed, edible ice cream cups measuring 1¼" at
    the base
6 pointed ice cream cones
1 large graham cracker cube (p. 18)
3 small graham cracker cubes (p. 22)
14 single graham crackers
thin rope licorice
1 package pointed gumdrops and other assorted candies for
    decoration
double recipe Royal Icing (p. 15) Reserve about ½ cup to tint
    in contrasting colors for flowers, and tint the rest of it
    pink.
3 or 4 chocolate candy bars to cut up as windows
tray, wooden board, heavy cardboard, or other sturdy sur-
    face at least 12" x 12" (on which to construct castle)
dull knife (for spreading icing)
sharp knife (for cutting licorice)

straight pins
decorator's tube

Towers

1. Using Royal Icing, glue 12 single graham crackers together in pairs to make 6 double-thickness crackers to
   use as bases for 6 towers.
2. Make each of the 6 towers with a stack of flat-bottomed
   ice cream cones topped by a pointed ice cream cone.
   Begin each tower with a flat-bottomed cone glued upside down on the graham cracker base and then add an
   upright cone, alternating upside down and upright
   cones as you proceed. Make the 6 towers as follows:
   • 2 towers consisting of 2 flat-bottomed cones and 1 pointed
   cone

- 3 towers consisting of 3 flat-bottomed cones and 1 pointed cone
- 1 tower consisting of 4 flat-bottomed cones and 1 pointed cone.

Assembly

1. Set 1 large graham cracker cube hollow-side down on a tray or other sturdy surface (see Figure 1).
2. Set 1 small graham cracker cube, hollow side forward, in the center front for an entrance to the castle (see Figure 2).

Figure 1   Figure 2

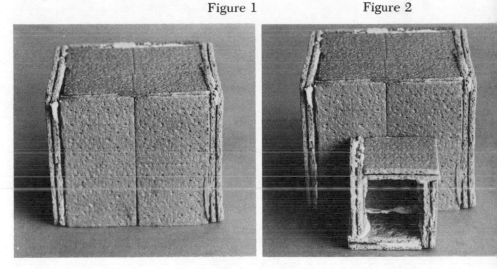

3. Set 1 small graham cracker cube to the far right for a low tower.
4. Set 1 small graham cracker cube on the main part of the castle at the front left as a support for an ice cream cup tower.
5. Set a small (2-layer) ice cream cup tower on the small graham cracker cube that rests on the large graham cracker cube (see Figure 3).
6. Assemble the rest of the towers around the castle to achieve the effect you want. Memorize the arrangement (see Figure 4).

Figure 3

Figure 4

7. Glue 2 single graham crackers together as a drawbridge for the entrance.

Decoration
1. Remove the towers from around the castle and apply a thin glossy consistency of pink Royal Icing to all surfaces.
2. Reassemble the parts of the castle while frosting is still moist so they will adhere to one another. Work quickly to complete the next procedures before icing hardens.
3. Cut chocolate candy bars for windows and stick on castle walls and towers.
4. Set pointed gumdrops around all flat ledges.
5. Add assorted candies as desired. Let icing dry.
6. Add flowerets and icing from a decorator's tube.
7. Cut 2 lengths of rope licorice as chains for the drawbridge and attach with straight pins from the top sides of the entrance to the far side of the drawbridge.
8. Cover the pins with swirls of frosting from the decorator's tube.

Caution: Remove straight pins if the castle is to be eaten.

Three times as big and elaborate as most gingerbread houses you see, this graham cracker structure is no more difficult to make because it is assembled from 3 large graham cracker cubes. However, the size of the structure is so large that it requires several boxes of graham crackers and can cost you up to $10 or more, depending upon the ornamentation you use. You may therefore prefer to build just 1 section of the 3-section house, in the more traditional manner of making gingerbread structures.

Another problem is that large graham cracker cubes do not hold up well in excessively humid climates or in buildings cooled by evaporative air conditioners. For safety's sake, make your large graham cracker cubes two or three days in advance to see if they retain their shape before proceeding with the entire structure. See *Effects of Humidity*, p. 18.

Materials needed for 3-section cookie house:
3   large graham cracker cubes for main structure of house (p. 18)
79 double graham crackers for roof, patio, etc. (This is in addition to the 60 double graham crackers needed to make the 3 large cubes. Because many of the crackers in any given package will be broken, you must purchase enough boxes to provide 139 unbroken double graham crackers.)

3   recipes of Royal Icing for assembling structure and covering it (p. 15)

assorted candies

tray, wooden board, heavy cardboard, or other sturdy surface at least 12″ x 14″ (on which to construct house)

dull knife (for spreading icing)

serrated knife (for cutting crackers)

ruler

cutting board

decorator's tube

5″ x 5″ Double-thickness crackers (for roof, patio, etc.)

1. Spread 1 double graham cracker with Royal Icing and set it on a working table.
2. Spread another double graham cracker with Royal Icing and set it on the table next to the first cracker, with sides touching.
3. Lay 2 more double graham crackers on top of the first 2 in the opposite direction (sides touching) so that you have 1 large double-thickness cracker measuring 5″ x 5″.
4. Repeat steps 1, 2, and 3 to make 18 more large crackers (19 in all) for roof supports. Let dry at least 1 hour before proceeding.

Assembly

1. Set 1 large graham cracker cube hollow side down on a tray or other sturdy surface.
2. Set 1 large graham cracker cube directly in front of the first, lining the sides up evenly.
3. Set another large graham cracker cube directly to the right of the first, lining the sides up evenly.

177

Roof supports

1. From the 5″ x 5″ double-thickness crackers you prepared earlier, cut 4 triangles as shown below.

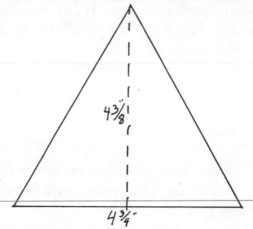

4 3/8″

4 3/4″

2. Using Royal Icing, glue the 4 triangles together in pairs
   to make 2 triangles with 4 thicknesses.
3. Glue the 2 triangles upright on the right and left edges of
   the first graham cracker cube.
4. From the 5″ x 5″ double-thickness crackers cut 8 triangles as shown below.

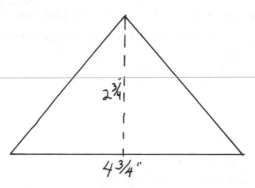

2 3/4″

4 3/4″

5. Glue the 8 triangles together in pairs to make 4 triangles
   with 4 thicknesses each.
6. Glue the 4 triangles upright on the right and left edges of
   the 2nd and 3rd graham cracker cubes. Let dry.

Roof

1. Glue a 5″ x 5″ cracker as one side of a pitched roof by setting it on the roof support of one section of the house.
2. Glue 5 more large crackers in place on the roof.
3. Make chimney as desired with graham cracker scraps.

Patio

Set a 5″ x 5″ graham cracker horizontally on the tray in the space created by the L-shaped house construction.

Steps

1. Glue 2 single graham crackers together one on top of another and fit them into the corner space. This makes the first step for the house door.
2. Cut 1 single graham cracker in half along the scoring and glue the halves together in a double thickness.
3. Set the half cracker on top of the whole cracker as the second step for the house door.

Railing

Glue 2 single graham crackers together one on top of another and set them upright against the steps.

Decoration

1. Cover the entire house assembly with a thin glossy mixture of Royal Icing.
2. Cut chocolate bars into pieces for doors and windows and attach them to house before icing dries.
3. Add other candies as desired while frosting is still moist.
4. Let icing harden and add other flowerets and icing trim with colored icing from a decorator's tube.

Merry-Go-Rounds (Large and Small)

A maxi merry-go-round in the middle and a mini merry-go-round at each place mean a merry, merry occasion for all!

Materials needed for 1 large merry-go-round:
1 candy stick 10″ high and ⅝″ in diameter
8 candy sticks 5 ¾″ high and ⅜″ in diameter
8 vanilla wafers
8 large animal crackers
8 small gumdrops
1 large gumdrop
Royal Icing (p. 15)
3 cardboard circles 12″ in diameter cut from corrugated
   paper
white paper or foil
heavy yarn—about 2 feet
8 pieces of ribbon about ½″ wide and 8″ long
scissors
pencil
knife
compass or round object for tracing
8 short straight pins
glue
decorator's tube

Base
1. Cut 3 cardboard circles of corrugated paper 12″ in
   diameter.
2. Glue the circles together.
3. Cover with white paper or foil.

Center pole
1. Cut a hole in the center of the base about ½'' in diameter.
2. Glue large candy stick in hole with Royal Icing. Let dry.

Outer poles
1. Cut a hole in the center of each vanilla wafer the diameter of a small candy stick.
2. Place wafers evenly around cardboard base about ¾'' in from edge and trace around edges and center holes with a pencil.
3. Remove wafers and make holes in cardboard to accommodate candy sticks.
4. Glue vanilla wafers and small candy sticks in place with Royal Icing and let dry.

Decoration
1. With Royal Icing and a decorator's tube put rows of icing around large and small candy sticks to help anchor them in place.
2. Put a row of decoration around each vanilla wafer.
3. Put a border of icing around the entire base.

Top
1. Put a dab of icing on top of each small pole and string yarn from pole to pole, sinking it in the icing. Connect raw ends of yarn.
2. Cut a hole ½'' in diameter in bottom of large gumdrop and glue it to top of center pole with Royal Icing.
3. Stick pin through end of each piece of ribbon from wrong side and stick it up through bottom of center gumdrop. Attach pins so ribbons are evenly distributed around gumdrop and pins don't show.
4. Bring other end of each ribbon down and glue it to the

front of corresponding small pole. (Ribbon should over-lap pole about 1'' below yarn.)
5. Cut tips off small gumdrops and glue with Royal Icing to top front of each pole to hide glue on ribbon.

Animals
Using Royal Icing, glue large animal cracker to the outside of each small pole at varying heights.

Caution: Remove straight pins if the merry-go-round is to be eaten.

Materials needed for 1 small merry-go-round:
1 sea toast wafer 4 1/4'' in diameter
5 candy sticks about 3/8'' in diameter and 3'' long
5 mints or round flat candies 1'' in diameter
1 candy stick about 1/2'' in diameter and 5'' long
5 animal crackers
1 small gumdrop
Royal Icing (p. 15)
colored paper
pencil
small piece of cardboard
decorator's tube
scissors
knife
glue
compass or round objects for tracing

Outer poles
1. Cut small indentation in center of each mint and glue small candy stick upright with Royal Icing. Let dry.
2. Using Royal Icing, glue candy sticks and poles around edge of wafer, evenly spaced. Let dry.

Center pole

Cut small indentation in center of wafer and glue large
candy stick upright with Royal Icing. Let dry.

Top

1. Cut circle of colored paper 6 ¼'' in diameter.
2. Cut from outside of circle to center.
3. Overlap slashed edges until you achieve the look of a
   pointed canopy. Glue in place.
4. Scallop edges of canopy with scissors, if desired.
5. Cut a round piece of cardboard 1 ¾'' in diameter.
6. Cut a hole the size of the candy stick (about ½'' diameter) in center of cardboard.

7. Glue cardboard inside center of canopy.
8. Set canopy on top of center pole and glue gumdrop on top.

Animals
Glue animal cracker to each of the 5 poles at varying elevations.

Decoration
Trim outer edge of merry-go-round with Royal Icing from a decorator's tube.

Index

189

About the Authors

Barbara Williams holds an M.A. degree from the University of Utah, where she taught English for twelve years. She is the author of two college textbooks, three plays, numerous magazine articles and over twenty children's books including *Albert's Toothache*, an American Library Association Notable Book for 1974, the popular cookbook *Cornzapopin'!* and the crafts book *Pins, Picks & Popsicle Sticks*. Ms. Williams, a mother and a grandmother, is married to a professor of political science. She and her husband make their home in Salt Lake City, Utah.

Rosemary Williams finds her entire life consumed with caring for her husband and five cookie-eating children. She studied at the University of Utah, then married and became a cook, candymaker, seamstress, homemaker and mother. Although her mother and grandfather were both writers, this collaboration with her sister-in-law on *Cookie Craft* is the first effort for her in the literary field. Ms. Williams and her family live in Salt Lake City, Utah.